McClure

ANTEBELLUM COLONIAL TENEMENT APARTMENT ESTATE CASTLE BACK-TO-BACK SUBURBIA

World Geography

Homes

of the world & the way people live

Atlantic Europe Publishing

THATCH WOODEN HOMES   STONE HOMES BRICK HOMES

How to use this book

There are many ways of using this book. Below you will see how each page is arranged to help you to find information quickly, revise main ideas or look for material in detail. The choice is yours!

On some pages you will find words that have been shown in CAPITALS. There is a full explanation of each of these words in the glossary on page 63.

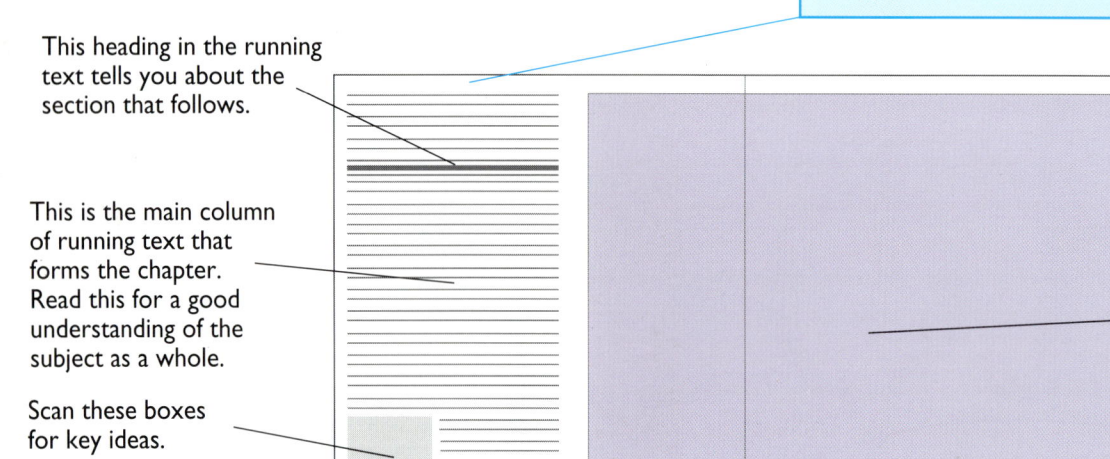

This heading in the running text tells you about the section that follows.

This is the main column of running text that forms the chapter. Read this for a good understanding of the subject as a whole.

Scan these boxes for key ideas.

The information in the box describes an important subject in detail and gives additional facts.

Author
Brian Knapp, BSc, PhD

Educational Consultant
Stephen Codrington, BSc, PhD

Art Director
Duncan McCrae, BSc

Editor
Elizabeth Walker, BA

Illustrator
David Woodroffe

Designed and produced by
EARTHSCAPE EDITIONS

Print consultants
Landmark Production Consultants Ltd

Printed and bound by
Paramount Printing Company Ltd

First published in the United Kingdom in 1994 by Atlantic Europe Publishing Company Limited, 86 Peppard Road, Sonning Common, Reading, Berkshire, RG4 9RP, UK

Copyright © 1994
Atlantic Europe Publishing Company Limited

The Atlantic Europe Publishing logo is a registered trademark of Atlantic Europe Publishing Company Limited.

Suggested cataloguing location

Knapp, Brian
    Homes of the world & the way people live
    – (World Geography; 2)
392.3

ISBN 1-869860-38-1

All rights reserved. No part of this publication may be reproduced, stored in a retrieval system, or transmitted in any form or by any means, electronic, mechanical, photocopying or otherwise, without prior permission of the Publisher or a Licence permitting restricted copying issued by the Copyright Licensing Agency Ltd, 33-34 Alfred Place, London, WC1E 7DP.

Acknowledgements
The publishers would like to thank the following for their help and advice: Aspen Flying Club, Englewood, Colorado; Terry Barringer, Royal Commonwealth Society Library, Cambridge University; Bendigo Aviation Services, Bendigo, VIC, Australia; Bridgeford Flying Service, Napa, California; Mathew Cherian, Oxfam-Bridge, India; Duncan and Jeane Cooper; Eveland Aero, Honolulu, Hawaii; David Newell, Oxfam-Bridge, Thailand; Victor Oh and Paramount Printing Co., Ltd and Wycombe Aviation

Picture credits
(c=centre t=top b=bottom l=left r=right)
All photographs are from the **Earthscape Editions** library except the following: **Stephen Codrington** 59tl, 59tr; **Jack Jackson** 4/5, 12c, 51b; **Leeds City Libraries** 32b; **Panos Picture Library** 8t (*Penny Tweedie*), 22/23 (*Rob Cousins*), 44/45 (*Jeremy Hartley*), 52/53 (*Sean Sprague*); **Royal Commonwealth Society Library** 53t; **The Sutcliffe Gallery** 35t; **University of Reading, Rural History Centre** 34, 35b; **Tony Waltham** 24tl, 56b, 57c; **ZEFA** 9b, 31t, 53br, 56c.

This product is manufactured from sustainable managed forests. For every tree cut down at least one more is planted.

2 CONTENTS

Contents

Chapter 1
Facts about homes and houses 5
Affording a home 6
How homes are used 6
Choices in home size and design 6
Homes and families 8
Inside the modern home 8
Changes in the industrial world 10
Apartment blocks 10
Changes in the developing world 12
Buildings for hot climates 12
Mobile homes 14
Houses that respect the environment 14
Timber homes for cold forest lands 14
Thatch and turf 15
The future of the world's homes 16
Homes of stone and brick 16
Self-build homes 18

Chapter 2
Revolutions in housing 21
The first city homes 22
Clues that tell of ancient homes 22
Differences between East and West 24
Homes that could be defended 24
Change in an age of trade 26
Patterns of historic houses 26
Merchant homes of success 26
New houses in the country 28
Historical settlements 28
Houses to suit city life 30
Farmhouses appear in the countryside 30
Homes for factories 32
Homes of the Industrial Revolution 32
Homes of the electrical age 34
Housing in the age of public transport 34
The modern suburbs 36
Commuters in the country 36
The motor suburbs 36

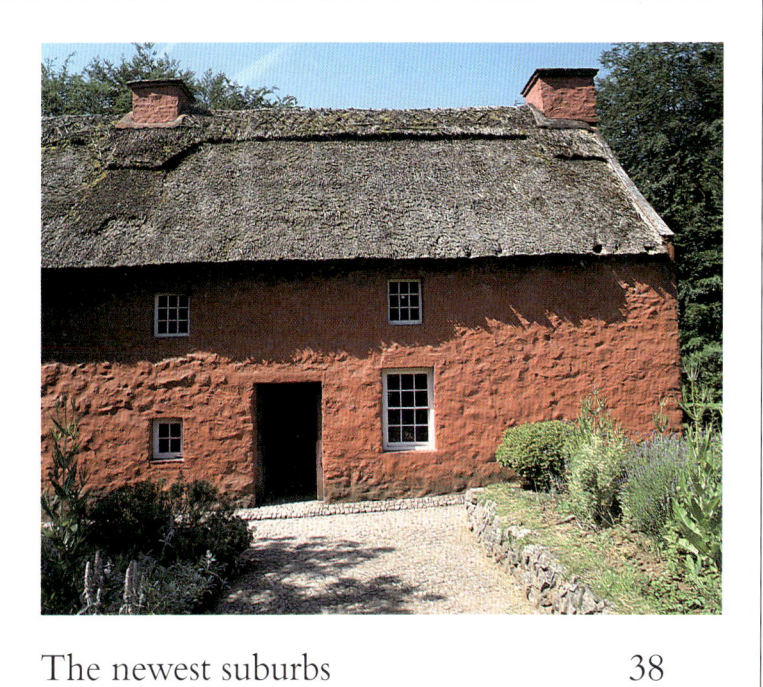

The newest suburbs 38
The need for social housing 42
Homes for all 42
Country homes 42
Mass production of homes 44
Social housing 44
Housing the future world 46

Chapter 3
Homes of the world 49
Africa and the Middle East 50
Homes in Africa and the Middle East 50
Latin America 52
Contrasts in Latin America 52
The United States and Canada 54
Varied frame homes in North America 54
Asia 56
Asia, coping with billions 56
Australia and New Zealand 58
Australian Homes 58
Europe 60
European homes: mixing old and new 60

Glossary 63

Index 64

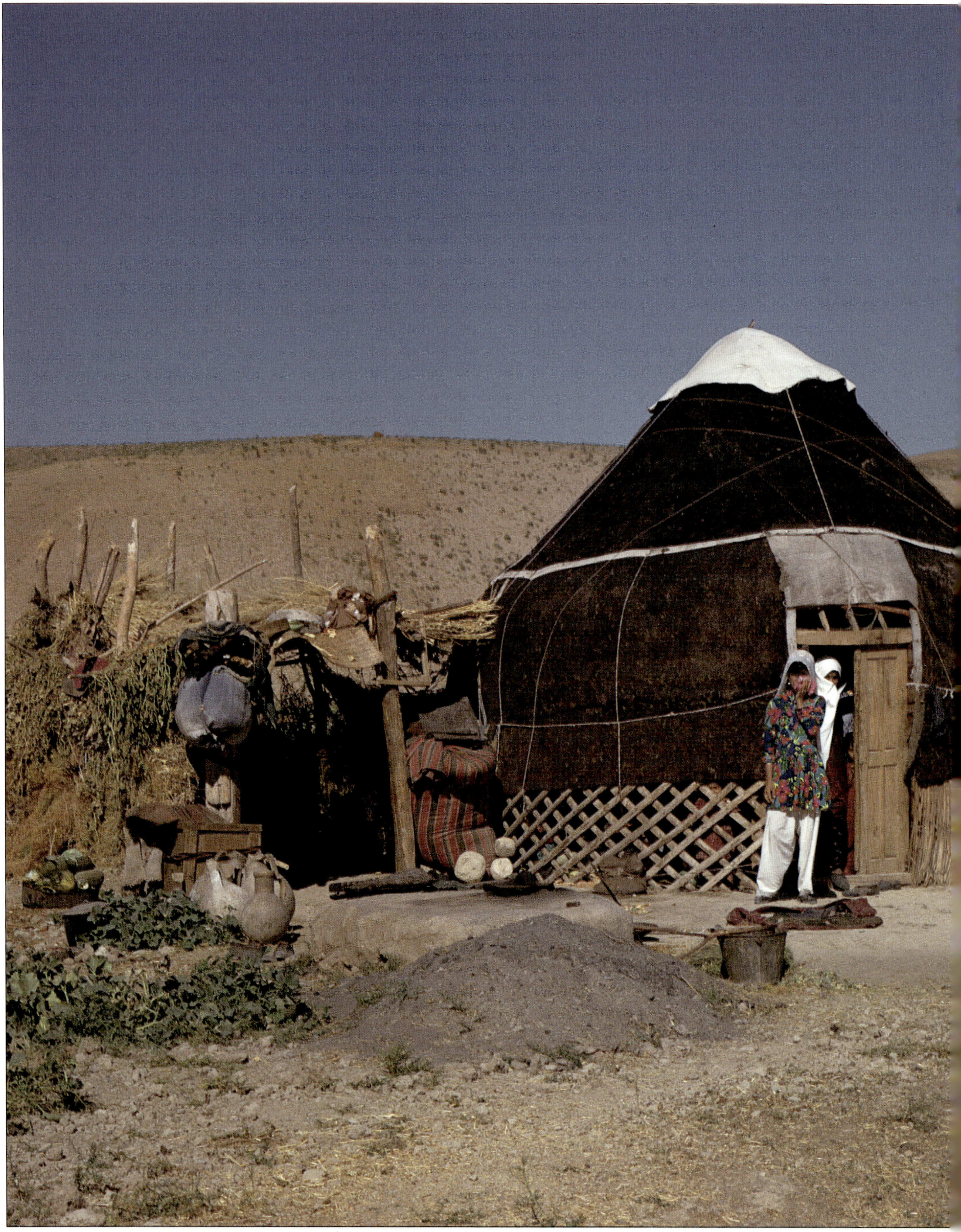

Chapter 1

Facts about homes and houses

The world contains five and a half billion people, by the middle of next century it may have ten billion. To find homes for all of these people will be the most expensive task the world has ever seen. It will be made even harder because people demand better homes with more space than in the past. It is a formidable challenge.

People spend more time in and around their homes than anywhere else during their lives. Throughout the world homes have become the single most important – and expensive – item in everyone's lives. It is now common for a quarter to a half of the family wages to go on the home, paying rent, paying back the loan used to buy the house or paying for repairs. In fact a greater proportion of the family wage is spent on paying for space in the poor slums of India than it is in the smart suburbs of the Sydney, Los Angeles or London.

So much money is invested in homes, and so many houses are needed in the world, that building and repairing them is also one of the world's leading occupations. But homes are not just piles of building materials. To make a house

❒ (left) A home is important because it gives a base to return to. Homes may vary from the palatial to the simple, from the ordinary to the bizarre. Homes also have to suit their environment. This Yurt tent, or Ooy, in Afghanistan, for example, is used by a nomad family. It has to be easily moved, and it must keep the family warm in winter and keep off the heat of the sun in summer.

FACTS ABOUT HOMES AND HOUSES 5

a home people need water, electricity, sanitation (toilets) and roads. Indeed, homes take up by far the largest space of any use in a city and providing services for homes takes up much of a city's taxes.

Affording a home

Because homes are becoming more expensive, there is great concern everywhere to provide homes that people can afford. More people are homeless now than ever before, mainly in developing countries, but the sight of homeless people is becoming increasingly common in city streets of industrial countries as well.

> The hardest task is to build good quality homes that are also affordable for people with average and low wages.

In every country there are some people who can afford to pay for a home and some who cannot. It is the government's job to try to build SOCIAL HOUSING (sometimes called public housing) for those in need. In countries that have always relied on private landlords to rent affordable homes, social housing makes up just a few per cent of all houses. In some other industrial countries, Singapore, Japan and some in Europe, governments or non-profit making organisations have provided or subsidised many homes; in the former Communist countries of Europe governments provided *all* the homes at low rents.

Since the early 1960s more than two million housing units per year have been constructed in the former Communist countries of Europe. The quality is poor and the homes are very small with only basic facilities, but at least people have been housed.

How homes are used

What is a home? It might be a palace or a castle, an apartment high above the city, or a shanty hut or a slum. It may be a tiny space

Choices in home size and design

Homes are basically boxes to live in. The choices people make are therefore:
- How big to make the house (how big shall each room be, how many rooms shall there be)
- How big to make the plot it stands on
- Whether to add more rooms (boxes) on the groundlevel (and make a single-storey, single-family home) or whether to make a two-storey single-family home, an apartment block of several storeys or an even taller tower block.

All homes fit into these categories as shown here.

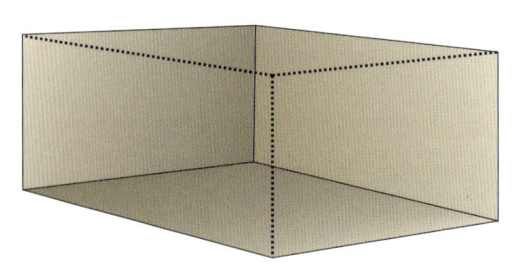

1 A home is a box-like unit for living in. Inside, it will possibly contain rooms for daytime use, bedrooms and additional rooms for cooking, bathing and so on.

2 Family homes can be made bigger by building boxes on top of each other. This is common in city suburbs where land is expensive but not in short supply.

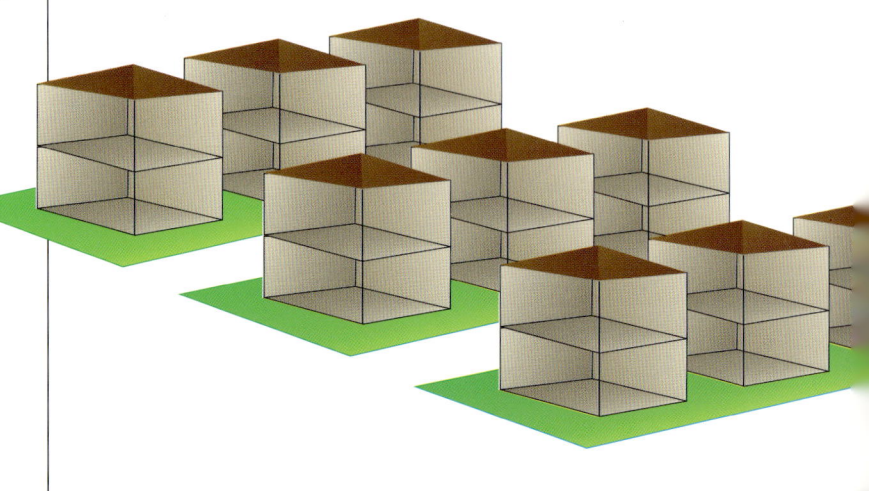

3 Tower blocks consist of many units stacked on top of each other. To make sure that the tower block is stable and will not fall down, the tower has to follow strict building rules. As a result tower blocks all look more or less alike.

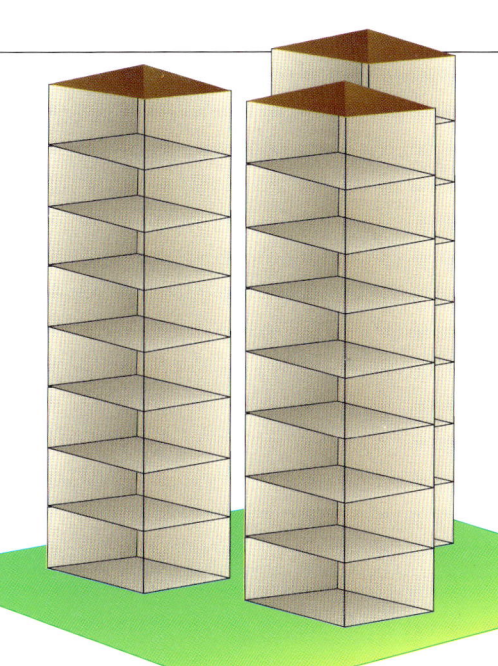

4 Apartment buildings are usually built up to five storeys high. The apartments are usually rented.

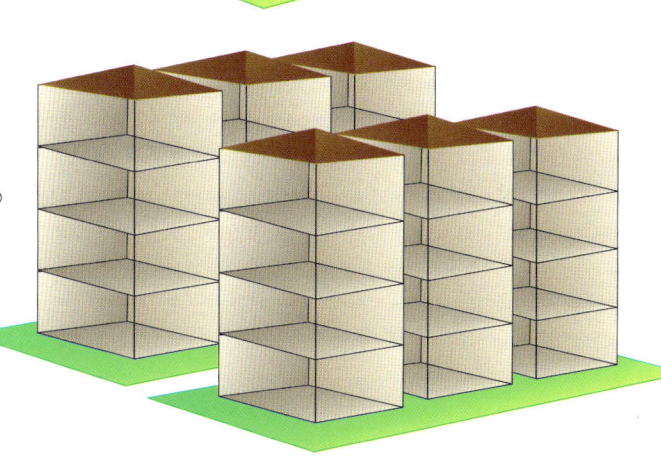

5 Townhouses are built side by side and share side walls. These are built where a there is a high density of people, such as in city centres where land is scarce.

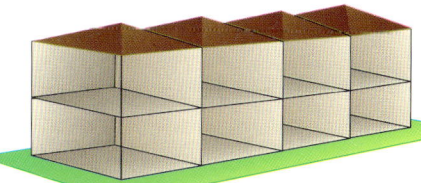

6 Single-storey family homes on large plots are built where people have private transport and where land is cheap and plentiful.

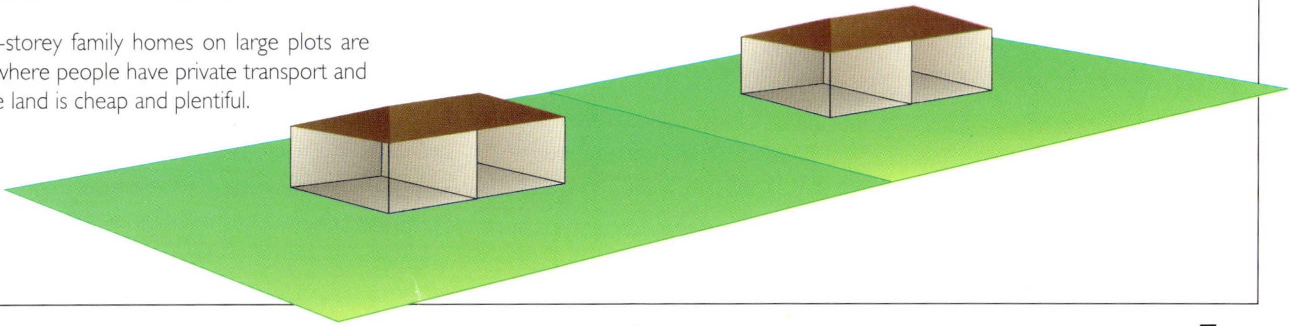

FACTS ABOUT HOMES AND HOUSES 7

just suited to one person or a communal longhouse where twenty people live. But no matter what its size, its location, or how many people share it, a home is a base, an 'anchor' in the busy world.

Because most people spend so much of their time at home, looking after the house is a major activity. A home has value and can be sold. A well kept home will have much more value than a poorly kept one. But houses are not isolated piles of brick and mortar. Most are grouped together into streets or crescents or some other pattern. In this way groups of homes make up neighbourhoods. A neighbourhood contains people who are friends as well as neighbours. If you want to sell your home, then buyers will not just want to know what your house is like, they will also want to feel comfortable in the neighbourhood.

> The single-family house is based on centuries of tradition modified by the latest ideas in fashion.

For these reasons neighbourhoods often contain people who think and behave in much the same way.

Homes and families

A home can be used for all manner of things. Of course homes are used for living in: sleeping, cooking and relaxing. But most people use their homes for even more. A writer may use her home as an office, a craft-worker may use his home for a workshop, people with collections may use their homes for museums, spare rooms may be used for renting to lodgers, and part of the house may even be used as a general store or a post office.

In most industrial countries, pressure on city space means dense housing, two thirds of all homes are single-family houses and the remaining third apartments, or houses divided up to be used by several families. In places

Inside the modern home

Homes throughout the world are surprisingly similar because everyone has the same needs. Inside, however, decoration and furniture reflect more traditional ways of life. For example, in a Japanese home people sit on the floor, there are few chairs and the table is very low. In homes in the Middle East, people prefer very sturdily built and highly decorated furniture. In the West people often prefer modern styles of furniture with simple lines.

Many modern homes are still built with living room, kitchen and three to five bedrooms. This has proved to be the most flexible design for all types of families. Smaller families can use any spare rooms as a playroom, a utility room or a study.

❐ (above) A family dining in Kuwait.

❐ (right) The main dining room for a family in Japan.

Facts about the house
Houses are made of several distinctive parts:
- A foundation
- A rigid frame to support the floors and roof
- A weatherproof surface.

It also has to contain services such as a water supply, sanitation, electricity and heating or cooling.

The whole stability of the house depends on a good foundation. Lightweight houses of bamboo or wood may be able to use a foundation as simple as a layer of stones. However, with brick or concrete the foundations must be stronger. Usually the soil is dug out and a slab of concrete laid to make the foundation. In places where there is frost, the slab must be protected from cracking by being well below the ground surface.

The house frame is bolted or concreted to its foundations so that it will not move even in severe storms.

The roof experiences the strongest winds and must be firmly fixed to the frame. The roof is usually made of wooden RAFTERS and the roofing surface is fixed firmly to these.

❏ (below) A wooden house on a large plot. The verandah provides a pleasant place to sit in fine weather, and protects the main entrance door when the weather is bad.

❏ (right) This diagram shows the main structure and rooms of a single-family house. The house has to have a wide range of services, such as running water and drainage, electricity and gas and possibly cable TV. These are all fed to the house from underground service lines and they are fed around the house through the wall and ceiling spaces. Most modern houses have central heating and/or air-conditioning. The hot water or cool air is fed in through the wall or floor spaces.

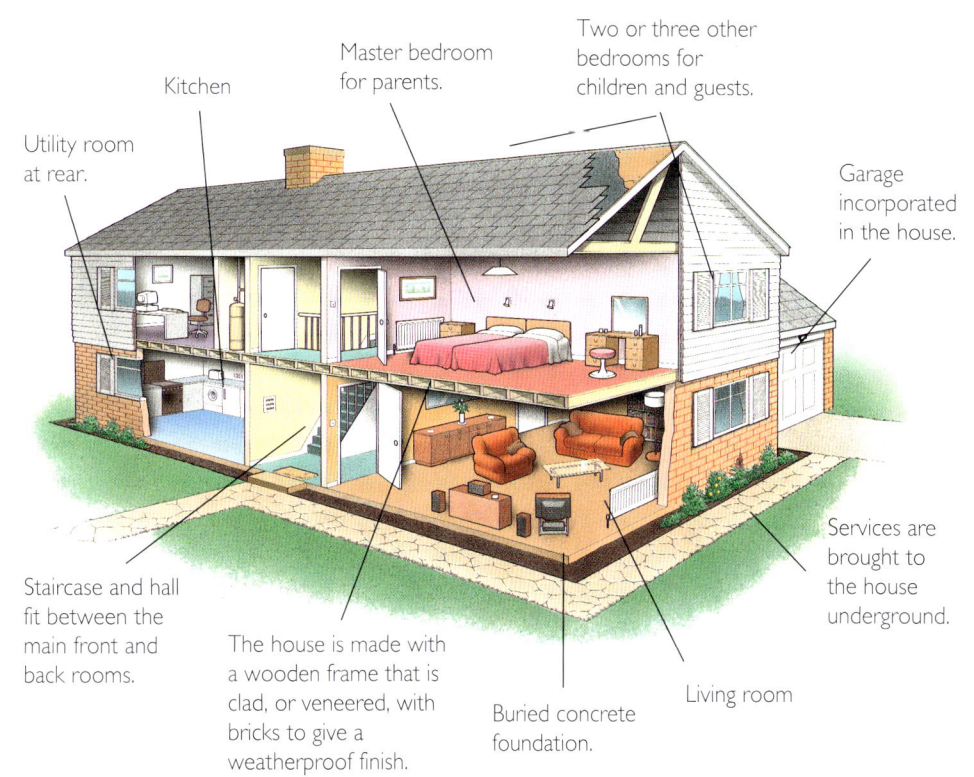

Kitchen

Master bedroom for parents.

Two or three other bedrooms for children and guests.

Utility room at rear.

Garage incorporated in the house.

Staircase and hall fit between the main front and back rooms.

The house is made with a wooden frame that is clad, or veneered, with bricks to give a weatherproof finish.

Buried concrete foundation.

Living room

Services are brought to the house underground.

FACTS ABOUT HOMES AND HOUSES   9

where there is less pressure in space, such as in Australia, the proportion of apartment blocks is much smaller.

But everywhere homes are remarkably similar in size. Four out of five of all homes, for example, have between four and seven rooms. However, the trend is to build houses with more facilities, such as a garage and a utility room. This means that the size of the average house is increasing.

Changes in the industrial world

The world contains about five and a half billion people who live together in groups of many sizes. The way people live depends on their background, their culture, how much money they have and the amount of space in the country where they live. But one thing is clear throughout the world: the need for homes is changing, because the size of families is changing quickly.

> The number of homes has to match the number of families. As families become smaller, a country will need more homes – even though the population may not be growing.

In the industrial countries, for example, the average age at which people get married, and the age at which they have children, has risen. It is now common for people to want to develop their careers and to save up money before they marry.

Newly married couples now tend to remain without children for longer, giving themselves more of a chance to save some money to support their children. And married couples tend to have fewer children than they did in the past, so that the average family now has only three members; half a century ago the average was four. Half of all families have no children at all.

Apartment blocks

An apartment block is usually built in a completely different fashion than a house. In an apartment block many families live in completely separate units. The block must therefore have enough space to allow several units to share each floor.

Because apartment blocks are more massive than houses, they need to have far stronger foundations. Modern apartment blocks are mostly built on long columns of reinforced concrete – called piles – that have been driven deep into the ground. A foundation raft of concrete is laid over the piles.

The modern tower apartment block is rather like a giant scaffolding frame with the spaces between the frame filled in with walls, ceilings and floors. The weight of the building is enormous, so the frame has to be especially strong.

Special shafts are provided in the centre of the building for elevators and services such as water, electricity and sanitation.

❑ (right) A common way of building apartments is to build them from the bottom up. These apartments do not use prefabricated pieces, and the whole building is constructed from the bottom up. Nevertheless, it is still basically a frame, with walls filling in the spaces between the frame. The crane sits on the upper floor and as the apartment block gets the higher, the crane has to be lifted as well.

☐ (left) Apartment blocks, such as these in Hong Kong, are much more exposed to the forces of nature than houses and they have to be designed to take hurricane force winds. If apartment blocks are built on sloping hillsides, special care has to be taken to make sure that the weight of the block does not cause the ground to fail and cause a disaster.

Facts about homes and houses

More people also choose to remain single whether or not they have children. Single people or single-parent families now make up a fifth of all households, far more than in the past.

All these changes have great importance for homes. It means that while the size of families has become smaller during the century, the number of people needing separate homes has become greater. So even in a country where the population is not increasing, there may be an enormous demand for more and more homes. On average, now, one new home is being built for every one and a half extra people.

> The home is the most flexible place in the world. It can be used for living, working and playing. Its size and shape depend only on the way people want to live.

Changes in the developing world

It always made sense for a poor family to share the cost of a home. Often, therefore, the number of people in a developing world home will be large, consisting of three generations: grandparents, parents and children. It is also common for several married families to live in one home. The families of several brothers, for example, may live in the family home. This pattern of living is called the extended family, and it is a time-honoured way in which people have supported each other.

But change is also happening in the DEVELOPING WORLD, at least for those whose living standards are increasing. As families become more wealthy, the younger members can afford homes of their own. So there is increasing pressure to split up the extended family.

Buildings for hot climates

In the tropics people do not have to worry about protecting themselves from the cold. Rather they need a shelter from the heat of the sun and possibly from torrential rainstorms. This has encouraged people to build homes that are light and airy in the humid tropics, often using naturally growing materials such as bamboo and palm leaf.

In the hot desert regions of the world bamboo and leaves are not available. The intense summer heat is best kept out with thick mud walls. Dried mud, known as adobe, is a good material in dry areas because it will last a long time without repair.

Adobe
This material, also known as mud-brick, is an amazingly flexible substance that has many advantages. It is simply mud mixed with grass or straw to hold it in place. It can then be formed into brick shapes and left to dry in the sun. It soon becomes rock hard. Alternatively it can be plastered on to a frame of sticks, to hold them together.

❐ (above) The thick adobe walls keep heat in during the winter and heat out in the summer. It is well suited to continental areas which have a dry climate.

❐ (above) These Moroccan homes are entirely made from adobe. They have few windows not just to protect themselves from the sunshine, but also from the threat of sandstorms.

❐ (below) Houses with hot climates are often built with verandahs. They provide shade and can be used as a kind of open-air sitting room.

Bamboo: grow your own house

This perennial grass grows widely in the tropics and it has been used to build homes since ancient times. It is easy to cut, its stems grow straight and, best of all, it will bend in the wind. In tropical areas that suffer from typhoons and other tropical storms, houses have to be able to withstand strong winds. Bamboo stands up better than most other cheap materials.

Many people grow their own houses; after harvesting, a clump of bamboo will have regrown within a few years and can be harvested again.

Bamboo is often split and used to make the walls as well as the frames of houses. Light walls of bamboo do not trap heat at night, and the gaps between the slats allow breezes to enter the home.

❐ (above) Bamboo.

❐ (left) A house made with palm leaves and bamboo.

❐ (below) A house made from thatch and bamboo.

FACTS ABOUT HOMES AND HOUSES 13

The result is an even greater demand for extra homes. It has forced governments to build tall apartment blocks in an effort to try to house people without producing sprawling cities.

Mobile homes

One recent trend in housing has been for people to buy mobile homes, which provide cheap housing. This is especially the case in the United States where many mobile homes have been laid out together in 'parks'. More than one in eight new homes built in the cities of the United States and one in four of the homes built in the countryside are now mobile homes, made of caravan materials but made to resemble a small house.

> Homes are becoming more expensive to buy and to rent. This forces the poorest people to live in old property or in flimsy mobile homes, or to set up shanty dwellings.

Mobile homes are flimsy, and they cannot stand up to severe weather like traditional lightweight homes built of natural materials in the tropics. For example, in the United States mobile homes always suffer badly when a hurricane or tornado strikes.

Houses that respect the environment

Today people are more concerned than ever to try to protect the environment. Homes affect the environment in many ways:

☛ They use raw materials from the ground, wood from trees and (as plastics) resources such as oil.

☛ They take up space once used by wildlife.

☛ Burning fossil fuels to heat and cool homes adds to the carbon dioxide in the air and thus to the Greenhouse Effect.

☛ They use up valuable countryside and reduce the world's wilderness.

Timber homes for cold forest lands

Much of the world was once forested. In the tropical forests most of the trees are hardwoods and difficult to use for house building. However, the conifers of temperate regions make ideal building materials. Timber is also warm and waterproof, so it provides good protection from cold wet winters.

The world contains a wide variety of trees, and almost all of them can be used for house building.

People making their homes from timber can choose to use logs that are simply notched at the corners and then laid on top of the other. This makes the walls and frame all at once. The great thickness of wood helps to keep the home warm in winter and cool in summer, but it is very wasteful of timber.

Log houses tend to used by people when there is wood in plenty. But most people use timber more carefully, sawing it into planks and using thick wood only for the main frame.

The best timber is wood that grows quickly (called softwood) because it can be worked easily. Softwoods are easy to saw, but they do not last as long as hardwoods. Thus many homes are built with hardwood frames and softwood walls.

Hardwoods are used for frames in many old houses. The style of the home usually showed the main timbers. Some houses made of wood have lasted over a thousand years.

Turf and thatch

People need a watertight roof for their homes and they have tried all manner of ideas. In cold areas such as Norway, traditional style roofs are made of planks and then covered in slivers of birch bark stripped from trees. The bark is then covered with soil to hold the bark in place. The soil roofing also helps to keep the heat in during the long cold winters. A healthy growth of grasses and flowers soon forms on the soil, helping the house to blend into the landscape. These are called turf roofs.

Thatch is the name for a thick blanket of reeds laid across a roof. It may need up to half a metre of thickness to make sure no water gets into the home, but a blanket of this kind is a natural energy saver, because it helps keep the heat inside during winter.

❐ (above) Timber is a commonly used material where houses are built in natural forest lands

❐ (above) Older houses often have exposed beams so that you can see how the frame has been made. This house also has a thatched roof made from marsh reeds.

❐ (below) These alpine houses are a combination of modern concrete and traditional wood. The gently sloping roofs hold the snow and help to keep the house warm during the winter.

Of all these problems, it is easiest to tackle the problem of energy by building good insulation into each new home, and adding insulation to older homes. This saves money and energy because fewer resources and less fuel are used.

It is much harder to save the countryside because people like to have large plots of ground. But it is possible to build so that plots are next to one another and no patches of waste ground are left in between.

The future of the world's homes

There will be two different kinds of home living in the future. The countries of the industrial world, as it presently stands, have populations that are not growing very fast, and they will have land to spare for the extra homes that will be needed.

> Homes can be made so that the materials used to build them, and the amount of energy they use for heating and cooling, do far less damage to the environment.

☛ The trend in owning more than one home will continue, so that homes by the seaside or in the country will be occupied for just a part of the year, or owned between groups of people who visit their second home on a time-share system.

☛ People will seek homes that have more character, and the price of historic homes will rise.

☛ More people will move from the cities to the towns and villages, and many city homes may become unused.

In the industrial world populations will not rise, but more homes will be needed as families continue to break apart or as people choose to live alone. For those who cannot afford a place to live, city authorities have the task of using taxes to pay for social housing.

Homes of stone and brick

These traditional materials are used to make a large proportion of the world's homes. Bricks have been used more often because they are much easier to obtain than stone.

❐ (above) Notice that the rough surface of this stone-built house show the large boulders that were used to build it. The same kind of boulders make the wall in the foreground. The boulders were brought from distant mountains by glaciers.

Stone

Stone, quarried from solid rock, was the traditional material of the wealthy. Some ancient peoples hewed their homes inside the solid rock; but most preferred to quarry the rock and move it to where they wanted their home.

More than any other kind of house, stone houses tell of the land. Stone is so heavy that it cannot usually be carried far, so a region with sandstone houses will be underlain with sandstone rock, limestone homes will be built near to limestone rock quarries and so on.

Some stone, like slate and shale, breaks into plates which are used as slabs to build walls. Sandstone and limestone are the two most preferred stones for building, because they can be cut easily into blocks and other shapes.

Not all stones are suited to building. Chalk, for example, is a soft white rock that soon crumbles way. But the FLINT it contains is tough and stands up well to the weather. So people made walls of chalk rubble and then faced them with flint.

Stone was once blasted from a quarry, cut into blocks and then carried to the site. It was time-consuming and expensive and is rarely done today. Modern builders use cheaper, crushed stone which is taken from quarries and made into blocks in a factory, using cement as an adhesive. The blocks are called reconstituted stone.

❐ (right) Townhouses made of brick.

Brick

Bricks are probably the most widely used of all building materials for permanent homes. They are far more useful than the sun-dried bricks or adobe, because they will stand up to rain and frost.

Bricks are made from mud. They are fired (heated) in a special furnace (kiln), which drives off the moisture and causes chemical changes in the mud. When the heating is complete a brick is a hard, nearly waterproof material that will bear heavy weights and can be used for multistorey homes.

The most striking difference between bricks is the variation in colour from dark purples and strong reds to sand colours and even light grey. This is determined by the chemicals in the clay, and brick pits can sometimes be identified by the colour of brick that is made from their clay. However, not all types of clay make good bricks.

Individual bricks are bonded together using cement (mortar). A tall wall made of just one thickness of bricks is likely to topple over, so brick buildings usually have two walls side by side, each tied to the other with small butterfly-shaped pieces of wire. This 'double skin' also keeps moisture from the inner wall, and the air gap between the walls helps keep the house warm.

❐ (left) Brick apartments built over shops. The brick has been covered with a surface of plaster (render) and painted.

❐ (below) Country cottages made from a yellow sandstone.

FACTS ABOUT HOMES AND HOUSES 17

All these things may happen to homes in the industrial world countries because they have room to spare. But some countries, such as The Netherlands, have already had to put many of their people into apartment blocks because they have only a small amount of space. Yet this is nothing compared to the space problems that will exist in countries that now form the developing world.

> In the developing world city governments try their best to tackle the ever-growing problem of housing all their people. But lack of money means they must leave most of the home building to the people themselves.

☛ Here, as cities continue to grow, more people will have to live in tall apartment blocks so that cities will not sprawl out of control. This change in living is necessary, because it is very expensive to run water, gas and electricity lines across sprawling suburbs, and much easier to provide them in compact cities.

☛ In the future homes will be more and more difficult to buy. As land becomes scarce and building materials more expensive, many of the poorest people will find owning a home impossible.

People in the developing world know they have to look after themselves and do so remarkably well. Some of the poorest SLUMS have been transformed into neatly organised suburbs by the patient building of poor people.

In the developing world, the best way forward is for city planners to allow people to build for themselves. Governments can help by marking out the land for future roads and other services. Blocking the way of those desperate for a home will not solve anything, people will simply go elsewhere and try again. After all, what do they have to lose?

Self-build homes

The millions of people who cannot afford formal houses have to learn to build for themselves. But building this way takes time, because families have to work for most of the week and building can only be done in their free time.

The people who have recently moved to an area may build a temporary shelter of stone and thatch. But this will not provide a good permanent home.

People who are determined to improve the quality of their lives have to build with brick. They may only be able to afford a few bricks at a time, and the bricks may not be of the highest quality, but with a plaster finish the houses can be made to look very attractive.

Self-build homes have to rely on each family to understand how to build a safe house. They may be lucky and have friends who can advise, but if they tackle building with no skills they may be setting the scene for all kinds of disasters in the future.

A simple structure can be made in just few hours, but it is only the first step toward a proper home.

❐ (right) This is a SHANTY home, a simple one-room home made of materials scrounged from the city waste tips. Cooking is done using dried cattle dung.

18 FACTS ABOUT HOMES AND HOUSES

2. The way in which houses are built shows clearly in these pictures. The house above is only partly built. Notice that a balcony has just been added to the first floor, but the hut with the sheet-plastic roof is only a temporary measure until a proper storey can be built.

The house on the right shows what can be done with time. Notice the side wall shows that the way the house was built was just the same as the one on the left. To cover up the poor quality bricks a coat of plaster and some paint has been added.

3. A street scene in a self-build suburb of Delhi, India. Now that you understand how the buildings are constructed, the street can be seen differently. Whereas it may appear as a shambles of buildings falling down, it is in fact a district where everything is being built up.

For example, the stones that appear to be scattered about will eventually be made into a wall when enough have been gathered. The strange low 'wall' on the first floor of the house on the right is simply a pile of building materials waiting for the time when they can be cemented into a wall.

FACTS ABOUT HOMES AND HOUSES

20 REVOLUTIONS IN HOUSING

Chapter 2

Revolutions in housing

Homes are not just piles of building materials. Everything about them tells a story of people's love-affair with the home. Not surprisingly, therefore, the world has always had a huge variety of homes.

Changes in homes and their uses have been most striking during the last two centuries when all societies have been changing quickly.

Somewhere around eleven thousand years ago a few people set up camp on the borders of what are now Iran and Turkey. They lived in what was called Mesopotamia.

They decided that the fertile land near to a river was a good place to live. It had plenty of wild animals to hunt, a water supply and an abundance of plants to eat. So, instead of the tents made of hides that they had traditionally used, they decided to build more permanent homes.

To make each home, they first excavated a shallow round pit and lined it with the shattered rocks found at nearby cliffs. The rock made a foundation on which were built walls of reeds and mud (adobe, see page 12) and a roof of thatch shaped like a cone. They called the settlement Zawi Chenui.

In doing this they thought out all the features of a modern house: situation, building materials,

❒ (left) The Anasazi built this small township about a thousand years ago. It is sheltered from the weather by a huge shallow cave and its position high on a cliff ledge was good for defence. With limited space, the Anasazi had to build upwards, constructing these four-storey dwellings with baked mud bricks.

REVOLUTIONS IN HOUSING 21

foundations, walls, roof. Today we still use the same basic formula handed down through all those generations.

About four thousand years after Zawi Chenui was built, and countless round houses later, people in what is modern-day Israel began to modify the round hut design; houses became rectangular in plan. This shape made it easier to add one room onto another. In this way homes became places where different things went on in separate rooms. And when the first bricks were made, buildings became stronger and more long-lasting. Thus the hut became a house.

> When people first decided to live together in cities, they had to rethink the house and the way they lived together.

Three thousand years later the rectangular house with its many rooms changed again. The Sumerians gave the rooms a definite plan and built them around a courtyard. They had developed the idea of a private house, turned inward from the rest of the settlement. Houses have been private places in many societies ever since.

The first city homes

A city needs to be organised around streets so that people can get around. When the first cities were built, in what is now Iraq, a completely new kind of home was needed. Homes had to be closer together so that the city could stay a compact size, so the builders of the day chose to build upwards. Thus the two-storey house appeared in the desert cities of about four thousand years ago. Each home had an upper floor and a small enclosed courtyard where cooking could be done. Attention could now be given to decoration, paving the courtyard and adding a balcony and a staircase.

Clues that tell of ancient homes

The world's ancient homes were not built to last in the way that ancient palaces, temples and monuments were. Most have long since crumbled away, their materials used as the foundations for more modern structures.

Only occasionally do we see the remains of ordinary homes that may be a thousand years old or more. The examples that exist show an enormous range of skills. People building at the same time but on different continents, and even on different regions of the same continent, had quite different techniques as can be shown by the pictures on this page.

Because people lived such isolated lives, techniques and skills were not passed on quickly. People everywhere were learning how to make the best of their homes, and about materials and the way homes should be designed. Evidence tells us that the homes were rebuilt time after time to make them bigger or to correct some disadvantage.

❐ (below) The people who built the homes on this windswept part of Dartmoor in southwest England were pastoralists and they used to graze their animals on land that had been cleared. They probably even cultivated the thin soils.

Winters were harsh and they found that the best way to protect themselves was to dig a pit. Around the edges of the pit they built low walls and then placed upright poles, to support a roof, in the centre of the pit. The roof, probably made of a frame of sticks with a thatch of reeds over the top, gave the shelter to see them through the coldest weather.

Similar partly-underground dwellings are found in cold regions in Europe and North America, although their different peoples never met. In each case the people came up with the same solution of how to build a draught-proof shelter with the minimum of materials.

This site was abandoned when the climate changed and the weather became too severe for farming.

❒ (right) The shelters built in the forests of northeastern North America by the Native Americans show a simple use of products of the forest. These people were hunters and gatherers and they often moved from place to place. With such a lifestyle they had little use for a more permanent type of house.

❒ (below) Machu Picchu, Peru. This picture of the ancient city high in the Andes shows the ruined homes in the foreground. All the building are made of stone. Notice the fine working of the stone and that each block has been carved to fit together with its neighbours.

REVOLUTIONS IN HOUSING

Differences between East and West

While people in the Middle East were developing their cities, cities and homes were being developed quite independently in other parts of the world.

By four thousand years ago, China also had great cities, and in them the world's largest number of permanent homes. Homes were private affairs here, too. Chinese homes were hidden from outside view and were entered through a high wall leading to a courtyard, just as in Sumerian homes. As elsewhere in East Asia, Chinese homes had curved (concave) roofs with wide eaves that gave welcome shadow to the walls during the hot summers.

> Each continent developed its own building styles to match its needs. In Europe, for example, the Roman Empire produced the first classic designs for homes. When it collapsed and lifestyles changed, Europeans had to re-invent the home.

But by this time a difference had developed between East and West that was to have an enormous effect on the way people viewed their homes. In the East people thought of their homes simply as places for living, not as a sign of wealth. They did not feel that the home needed to be permanent and they took little interest in the appearance of the home. Thus, once a satisfactory style had been developed, it was copied down the centuries.

In contrast, in the West people began to see homes as something of value to be preserved. For the wealthy, it became of great importance to be able to build bigger homes that were more modern in style and more costly than their neighbours' homes. They added, they enlarged, they decorated, and as a result homes

Homes that could be defended

Traditionally the wealth of a country was in the land, and the wealthy marked their good fortune by building grand homes among their estates.

But life was not secure, so homes were built for defence as well as for shelter. Fortified towers, called keeps, were surrounded by walls and battlements to make castles. Essentially, however, the keep remained a home, with bedrooms and a large living space or hall.

❐ (above) The fort at Delhi, India was one of the world's largest defended homes. It was built by the Moghul rulers who originally came from what is now Uzbekistan.

24 REVOLUTIONS IN HOUSING

Classic homes of the past

Reeds, like other naturally flexible materials like bamboo, lent themselves to experiment. Soon it became clear that arches and columns could be made of these materials, and that they could be made into a frame for the walls. Rooms could be bigger when the roof was supported with columns. Doors could be made if they were held up by frames consisting of two posts and a cross beam (lintel). And a lintel could be used to support an opening in the wall: a window. Mesopotamia was the birthplace of the first houses with columns. It happened nearly 4000 years ago.

The Greeks, and later the Romans, so famed for their majestic architecture, used the ideas of Mesopotamia for their own homes as well as their grand temples and other buildings. The Romans began to design each room of the house for a specific use. Thus they had separate bath houses and kitchens. They also built their homes in different parts of the cities than where they worked. In this way they invented the residential district.

The most powerful and wealthy could afford to build gigantic homes called villas. But most people earned low wages. To cram them into the city the Romans devised the world's first apartment blocks (which they called *insulae*). Rising up to five stories, they consisted of small, bare and uninteresting rooms which were designed simply to be slept in. Many people shared each sleeping room, just as they shared the outside kitchens, baths and latrines.

❐ (below and right) In medieval Europe the symbol of power and wealth was the home. The ultimate home was the castle, often protected by a water-filled ditch, or moat. The bigger the castle, the better it showed the owner's high place in society. These pictures are from England and Italy, respectively.

REVOLUTIONS IN HOUSING

became a central part of western life. This difference in attitude explains why ancient homes of the East have not been preserved, yet so many remain in the West.

Change in an age of trade

The age of trade would change the world's homes forever. People would begin to see the styles that had been developed around the world, and they would begin to alter and to copy from others, to mix and match to suit their wealth and tastes.

The age of trade was also a time when people from Europe began aggressively to dominate the world. It was the start of the age of worldwide empires. Empires were nothing new: the Greeks, the Romans and the Mongols had all developed great land-based empires. But the sea-based empires took house styles from one continent to another in the space of a few short decades.

In Europe, by the 15th century, the need for castles and fortified houses was not as great. Gradually the battlements and other fortifications disappeared; windows became larger and glass was invented, so that the house came to look more like they do today.

> In China, once a satisfactory style of home had been developed, it was copied down the centuries.

The Age of Discovery, and the era when European countries set out to colonise the world, was an important time. In those countries that were colonised, the original homes of the native peoples were either destroyed or their designs ignored. Europeans imposed designs from their homelands and the world became a far more uniform place.

Patterns of historic houses

In the past there were no city planners to supervise where each house was built. But historic settlements still worked well. The

Merchant homes of success

The period between the 16th and 18th centuries in Europe and America was a time of rapidly increasing wealth. Many became very prosperous and some merchants – people who traded goods – became fabulously wealthy.

Most wanted to express this wealth and success in the homes that they built for themselves, just as people had done by building castles and palaces in previous centuries.

But few now desired the enormous homes of the past; they preferred homes that were easier to live in.

❐ (above) A 17th-century city house with a walled garden in the United Kingdom.

26 REVOLUTIONS IN HOUSING

❐ (right) Substantial woodframe homes also tell of local success. This 17th-century house in New England (USA) could only be the home of someone who had become prosperous.

❐ (below) The wealthy merchants of Venice (Italy) advertised their success by building along the banks of the Grand Canal, where they could be seen by all.

REVOLUTIONS IN HOUSING 27

streets may wander about and the houses may be built touching each other, but they have an attractive charm that is missing in our modern planned settlements. So how did they manage?

The wealthier people in each settlement owned the land and each acted just like a private planning office. There were also recognised styles and building codes to follow, as laid out by the master builders. In other words, they did have a plan. They also had few homes to plan for, at least when the settlement began.

> Historically, populations grew slowly, so there was little pressure to build quickly. This gave time for each new home to fit into its place.

Each settlement had to contain all types of people, from the very wealthy to the very poor. The houses of the poor were not meant to last, and soon had to be replaced. But each replacement was built in the style of the time. In this way houses of a variety of ages and styles can be seen next to each other, forming part of the pattern of growth.

In the historic cities the bulk of the homes are often crowded in between the main public squares and streets. This is because the land was in the hands of the wealthy, who wanted their own homes to be grandly sited along the edges of the squares or lining the main streets. Everyone else had to pack into the spaces that were left. Today these grand and crowded places are tourist attractions such as London's Soho.

New houses in the country

The country had always been a place of villages and grand country houses. But changes in the city drove changes in the countryside as well. New schemes of farming were developed that meant farming could be done by family units rather than with the help of the whole village. In the colonies families were also

Historical settlements

In a country where people have to get around on foot or by using animals, it makes sense to keep travelling to a minimum. So for thousands of years people lived in compact settlements.

Wide streets wasted space, so usually the main ceremonial squares were the only open spaces. Otherwise houses jostled 'cheek by jowl', often being built many stories high to avoid wasting valuable ground space.

Most of the poorer houses have long since fallen down or been replaced with those made of brick. But the original street plans show where the homes were sited.

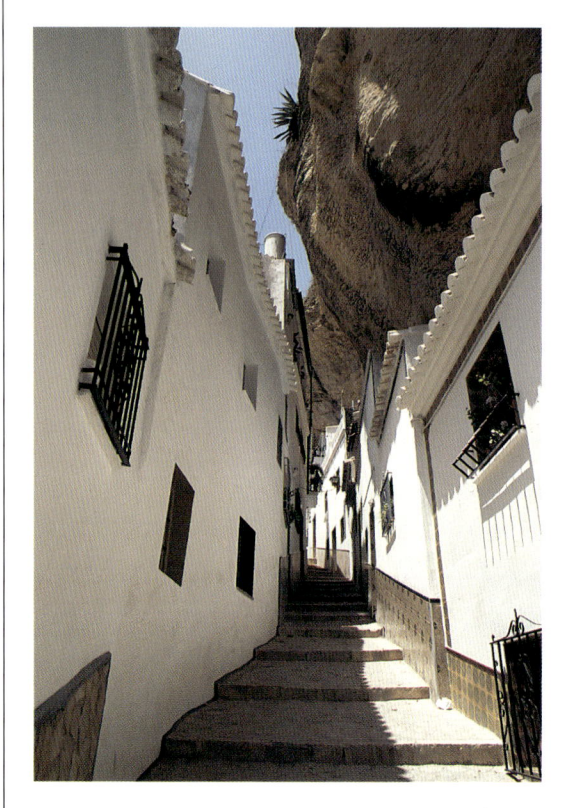

❐ (above) Narrow lanes were only meant for people or animals. The plan did not include space for modern motor vehicles. Notice how the homes have few windows facing the street. Those that do, the 'public' windows, are protected with grills.

Most people preferred to look out onto enclosed courtyards rather than onto the public street.

❐ (right) This hilltop village in Spain shows the main character of historical settlements. A larger city would have had the same basic arrangement.

The settlement is surrounded with open countryside, so there was no shortage of space. This means that people built their homes close to one another because they wanted to.

The high point of the settlement is the church, and the houses and apartments are built around it.

At one time it must have been important to protect the houses from attack, because there are the remains of a brown-coloured wall just below the church. The homes are painted white to reflect the hot summer sun away from them.

❐ (left) Enclosed gardens are a common feature of historic city homes. They offered a little privacy where homes were so closely packed.

The walls of the house and the garden are made of limestone. The large gates at the back of the garden suggest the it may originally have been the courtyard where horses and a carriage were kept.

❐ (right) Venice (Italy) is one of the world's most famous historic cities.

Although the city is on an island, it was not the shortage of space that caused people to build their homes so close together. They probably did so for the same reasons as the people in the Spanish village in the picture at the bottom of the page.

❐ (right) The Chinese were also city-dwellers and their homes, although compact, could be substantial. They were traditionally built around a courtyard.

REVOLUTIONS IN HOUSING 29

farming the land for the first time. This created the need for farmhouses, and the modest family home became a feature of the country landscape.

Houses to suit city life

At the start of the 18th century people across the world still built mainly for the country because few lived in towns and cities. City houses were simply copies of the country style. But by the 18th century, as cities grew more fashionable and more crowded, houses were replanned for the new age. The traditional single large room (hall) shrunk in size and became the foyer, the area near the entrance door. The house was divided into reception rooms, such as sitting rooms, built on a more friendly, human scale than in the past.

During the next century, people from Sydney to New York, Calcutta to London, Rio de Janeiro to Santiago consciously copied what they saw as the best in design. The Italian architect Andea Palladio influenced much of the colonial world with his new designs, creating a style known as Palladian which was carried to North America and Asia by the British, and to South America by the Spanish and Portuguese.

❐ (above) The traditional home in the country was the country house or stately home. This is a grand home, with dozens of rooms, a formal drive and gardens and surrounded by elegant parkland.

Farmhouses appear in the countryside

While dramatic changes were happening in city homes, equally sweeping changes were happening in the countryside.

Farmhouses are a new part of the countryside. They were not common before the 17th century. No-one lived alone in the fields for many practical reasons. People needed to cluster together to help each other in times of need and to defend themselves from attack. But most important of all, they didn't own the land they farmed.

The farmhouse appeared for two quite different reasons. When the pioneers left Europe and made their way to the colonies in Australia and North and South America, they found land that was not owned by landlords. So they were free to select their own patch of land and build their own house on it.

By contrast, farmhouses appeared in Europe as the old medieval system of feudal farming broke down. The land that had been owned for centuries by lords of manors was broken up and sold off. For the first time farmers found all their land in one manageable piece, not a collection of strips scattered over the landscape, so they had a reason for building their homes among their fields.

❐ (below) A farmhouse built by pioneers in Colorado (USA).

Pioneer farmhouses

As people colonised the Americas and Australia, their farmhouses were often very different from those of Europe. Pioneers got their land for free, so the farmers didn't have to be wealthy. Farmhouses therefore tended to be simpler than their European counterparts.

Of course, through hard work many pioneer farmers became more wealthy with time, adding rooms and other facilities to the original house. Others started all over again. In the southwestern United States pioneers borrowed the housing style from the Spanish Mexicans who borrowed it from the Spanish before them. Thus the RANCH was born.

❏ (above and left) A farmhouse in New Brunswick (Canada), shows their simplicity but also the care taken in construction.
❏ (right) A settler family listens to the 'wireless' in their mid-western farmhouse.

REVOLUTIONS IN HOUSING 31

Most important of all, houses were no longer built singly; in cities they were planned as rows, crescents and squares. Each house was given the same basic design, varying only in the shape of the doors and other details. From this time on people would try to make their houses look individual by concentrating on the furniture they used inside the home.

Homes for factories

It was the Industrial Revolution – that time between the 18th century and end of the 19th – when people moved from the countryside to the city in huge numbers. Also at this time people started to become slightly healthier; death rates went down and people started to live slightly longer. Each of these changes by itself would have caused homes to be rethought, together they caused a revolution.

As the new factories sprang up, people were needed to work in them. Since the factories had to go where there was water power or coal supplies – neither of which had been needed in such quantities before – there were usually no people nearby. Houses had to be built alongside the factories for the workers. In many cases this was how an industrial city grew up, from a factory and some houses to a city of millions within about a century.

> The need to build quickly and cheaply produced the industrial town, with thousands of small houses crammed together in a gridiron pattern.

Houses for workers had to be built quickly and cheaply. This meant that people could no longer plan to add a new house here, another there, like before. The factory controlled where and when the houses were built, and for the first time housing was planned.

The new houses had an enormous effect on the nature of the city. Because many people still had to walk to work, houses still had to be

Homes of the Industrial Revolution

The Industrial Revolution brought wave after wave of people from the countryside seeking jobs in the cities. None of these people were wealthy, so the only way they could be housed was by mass-producing modest homes.

The easiest and cheapest way to build houses is to build one house against the other, so that side walls can be shared. This gives a huge saving in building materials. The first homes of the industrial age were also built back-to-back, saving even more space and building materials.

When you build rows of little houses it is fastest and cheapest to build in straight lines. If you are building many houses at the same time, it is best if the roads are laid out in a simple plan. As a result these little industrial houses were mainly built in rectangular blocks, a pattern called a gridiron. In this pattern each straight road meets at right angles, and each housing block is about the same size.

When the Industrial Revolution began and cities expanded, they first contained rows or courtyards of small houses built beside factories. Many soon became slums.

32 REVOLUTIONS IN HOUSING

2 The way to squeeze more people into the same space was to replace the houses with taller buildings that could be divided up floor by floor. These were called tenements and the standard of living in them was usually appallingly low. These are shown in the picture below.

3 The style of building depended on local tradition. In Wales, Scottish mining areas, and in much of continental Europe, homes were built as tiny cottages.
This historic picture (above) shows coal burning in most houses in the Welsh mining valley of Ebbw Vale. You can see the way each street of cottages was built parallel to one another. The small structures in the foreground are the kitchens and toilets of the homes.

4 Most of the homes built during the industrial age were not mass-produced in the way we mean it today. Rather they were built in small numbers by the local builders. Each builder had his own style, so although he built onto the end of the houses already in each street the differences in style show through.

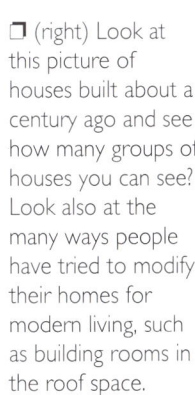

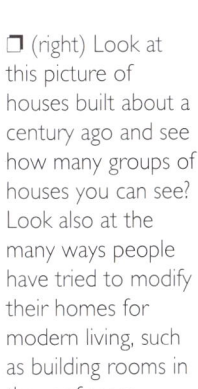

❏ (right) Look at this picture of houses built about a century ago and see how many groups of houses you can see? Look also at the many ways people have tried to modify their homes for modern living, such as building rooms in the roof space.

REVOLUTIONS IN HOUSING 33

built in a compact way. Thus they were built side by side and back-to-back so that each house could share two, and often three, walls. The long rows were often called terraces, and the homes terraced houses.

These tiny brick houses have stood up to the weather better than anyone ever intended. These are the buildings which, kilometre after kilometre, make up the old industrial world that seems so strange to people from newer countries like the United States and Australia. But early industrial housing, with its familiar terraces of houses, can be seen in many parts of New England (USA) and Victoria (Australia). Housing of this industrial age is often the most densely populated part of a city.

Homes of the electrical age

The invention of electricity allowed factories to be placed in much more varied sites by allowing them to use electrical machines, instead of those driven by steam engines or water. Electrical machines cause less pollution than steam machines and can be housed in quite different buildings.

> As public transport was developed, more people could live away from the city centre in the new suburbs, where houses were bigger and better built.

The kind of goods being made in the factories also started to change. For the first time, more goods were made for the home, and the home itself was being rethought to accommodate all the new electrical appliances that were coming onto the market.

The new home designs needed more space: for a washing machine and a refrigerator, for everyone to have their own bedroom, for a proper bathroom and toilet, for a garden, for a garage. And to match all of these changes, the houses of the twentieth century were built for people who were a little wealthier and who

Housing in the age of public transport

Nineteenth-century houses were built in terraces, separated only by narrow streets, because people mostly had to walk or use a horse and cart to get around. If houses had been made bigger, and the streets wider, then cities would have become bigger and it would be even harder for many people to get to work.

The first opportunity to change this age old pattern came with the development of the trams and the railway. As stations were built in the countryside, new 'towns' sprang up near them, adding to the edges of the city and creating the first suburbs. Los Angeles might seem like a typical motor town, but it actually spread out with the Red Line trams.

The invention of motorised transport allowed people to live away from tram and railway lines. Buses could visit many new areas. The homes lined the main roads in and out of the city, while at their backs was open farmland. These long strips of houses soon came to be known as ribbon development or highway housing.

❐ (below) The railway and tram car allowed people to live a little farther from the city centre, but they still had to walk to and from nearby tram stops or stations. Houses became bigger, but streets of houses were still designed to be as compact as possible.

◻ (left) This picture shows the long gardens and greater space that could be provided for districts served by public bus or car. The change from compact city to sprawling suburb was responsible for the huge expansion of most cities.

REVOLUTIONS IN HOUSING 35

could afford to have a home that was bigger and spaced farther apart from neighbours.

It was the new style of home that, more than anything, caused the cities of the industrial world to SPRAWL out into the surrounding countryside during this century. It produced the part of the city we now call suburbia.

The modern suburbs

Suburbia was mainly built in the motor age. It is the largest part of an industrial city, and it is made up almost entirely of private, single-family homes or low-rise, privately owned apartment complexes called condominiums.

Suburban houses are mainly built in the spaces between the main city roads. They occupy a maze of streets which are dominated by the single-family home. Houses are each set in their own garden, with room for a garage and, in places where the climate allows, a swimming pool.

The houses in suburbia are sometimes built in large estates; these are the work of large national construction companies, but most have been built individually, each small group the work of a small construction company.

> Electric power and the motor car changed the way people lived just as dramatically as the Industrial Revolution. Homes could be built with a garden and space for a car. In this way the suburbs were born.

Commuters in the country

As roads have improved, so more people are able to live away from the city. They still work in the city, driving back and forth each day. Such people are called commuters, and the countryside where they live is often referred to as commuter country.

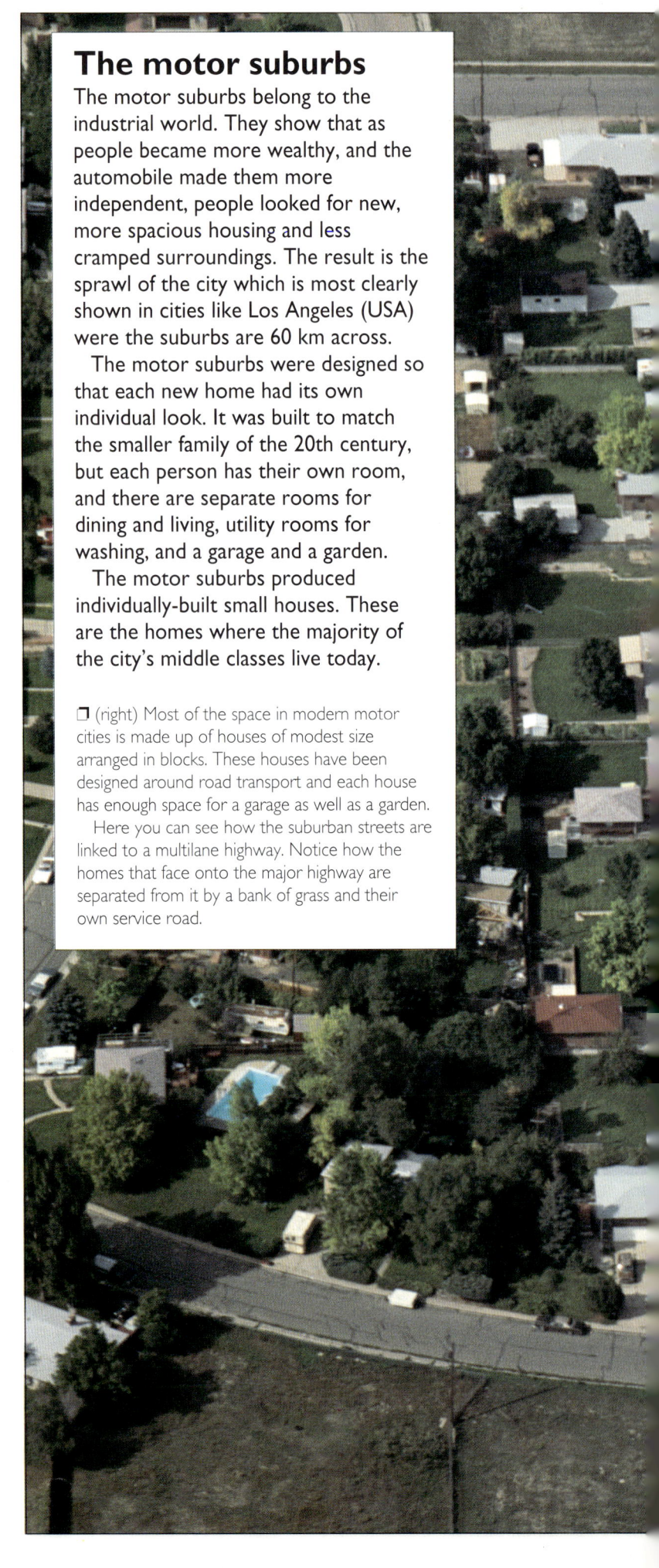

The motor suburbs

The motor suburbs belong to the industrial world. They show that as people became more wealthy, and the automobile made them more independent, people looked for new, more spacious housing and less cramped surroundings. The result is the sprawl of the city which is most clearly shown in cities like Los Angeles (USA) were the suburbs are 60 km across.

The motor suburbs were designed so that each new home had its own individual look. It was built to match the smaller family of the 20th century, but each person has their own room, and there are separate rooms for dining and living, utility rooms for washing, and a garage and a garden.

The motor suburbs produced individually-built small houses. These are the homes where the majority of the city's middle classes live today.

❐ (right) Most of the space in modern motor cities is made up of houses of modest size arranged in blocks. These houses have been designed around road transport and each house has enough space for a garage as well as a garden.

Here you can see how the suburban streets are linked to a multilane highway. Notice how the homes that face onto the major highway are separated from it by a bank of grass and their own service road.

Revolutions in housing

Commuter country used to be farmland; much of it still is. Many people value above all the chance to live in a quieter, more relaxed atmosphere than the city. Homes are larger and people can have larger gardens. The result is that a small number of people take up a large amount of space.

Many commuters like to have the benefits of the country but the convenience of living in a community. They choose homes that have been built on the edges of small settlements that have shops and other facilities.

Commuters' homes are away from the cities, so all the services that they need, such as water, electricity and sewage, cost more to install.

> The most recent suburban housing allows much more space for gardens, roads and pavements than the terraced housing of the inner city.
>
> Where the landscape allows, suburbs are built on hills, giving people views of the city.

The newest suburbs

The suburbs have gradually sprawled farther and farther into the countryside since they were first started in the 1920s. Of course, over this time, ideas have changed and the outer suburbs have different patterns of homes from those built many years ago.

The most striking thing is that the uniform rectangular blocks have given way to more interesting road designs, with curves and CUL-DE-SAC roads. The cul-de-sac fits inside the traditional block, making each block bigger, but still using all the space efficiently.

❒ (right and below) This is part of a housing pattern in the outer suburbs. Each of the houses is a detached single-family home. In back is a small area laid to lawn, while the front space has room for a second car or for visitors. Few cars are kept on the street. The cul-de-sacs provide quiet, safe, play areas for children.

Each of the homes shown here is built in a chalet style. You can clearly see the way the roofs have been designed with a split level, and the main garage is built inside the house.

❏ (right) People can chose to have any design of house they want. Many opt for traditional designs, such as showing exposed beams, a style copied from European homes of the 16th century.

REVOLUTIONS IN HOUSING 39

Because the homes are spaced widely apart, joining the services for all commuter houses also costs more. Even the roads have to be longer, because each house has a large frontage.

Some people choose their homes to be deep in the country. They know they will have to pay more for their electricity and sewage, but they choose to live in woodland or by rivers or even out in the desert. The nature of these homes varies enormously because they are all built individually or at most in small groups. In some places much of the woodland has been bought by home owners so that no one else can build there. In such places the countryside is really made up of very large private plots.

> The countryside is increasingly popular as people try to escape from the crowded, noisy city life. Homes in the countryside can be bigger and cheaper; but people may have a long drive to work each day.

❐ (above) These homes are almost new. They belong to people who have enough money for a large house. Many have garages made for two cars. Notice that more farmland is being cleared to make way for an extension to this suburb.

❐ (right) People have different lifestyles now than in the past and more people have free time from work and money to spend on luxuries. As a result they want their homes to be convenient for leisure. This picture shows how a housing complex is being built around a marina. The marina is excavated from farmland and connects to a nearby river.

40 REVOLUTIONS IN HOUSING

REVOLUTIONS IN HOUSING 41

Another group of people also lives in the countryside. These are the less well off people who have taken the opportunity of lower land prices to build their own houses, often in ramshackle fashion.

The need for social housing

Although many people moved out to new houses in the growing suburbs, many others remained unable to afford to buy their own homes.

The less well off traditionally rented houses, apartments, or perhaps only rooms from private landlords. But this left many people at a great disadvantage. They were often grossly overcharged and conditions could be very poor. Thus, early in this century, many governments began to try to offer a better deal by building homes and charging fair rents for them.

> While the well off are able to afford homes in the country, poorer people have to rely on social housing in the inner cities.

Apartment blocks were often built in large groups, or estates, and many were built on land that had once been used for old, poorly built factory houses. So, as the old homes were swept away and large estates of modern apartments took their place, sections of the world's older cities took on a completely new look.

Homes for all

The idea that the government should provide homes for all was important in all Communist countries. The leaders of these countries felt that all property should be owned by the state, not privately as it is in the West.

The main opportunity for the Communist regimes to build social housing came in Europe after World War II, when the governments had to rebuild their destroyed cities. It was also adopted in China as the authorities tried to house the city population.

Country homes

There are relatively few people who want to live in the countryside. Those who do are two very different groups of people: the wealthy, who want a lot of space around their homes; and the poor, who live in the country because it is cheaper than the city.

People who live in the countryside get the benefits of a quieter life, but they may not get all the convenience of city living. People here may be responsible for their own drives, they may not be connected to on-line drainage, and they almost certainly will not be able to get cable TV!

❐ (above) In the countryside some of the conveniences of the town will be missing.

❐ (below) The signs tell how the land has been developed privately, plot by plot.

❐ (above) It is still possible to live away from others in the countryside, as shown by this sprawling development outside Denver (USA). Compare this to the pattern of housing in suburbia on the previous page. What are the similarities and differences?

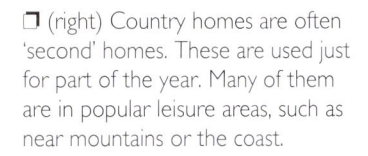

❐ (right) Country homes are often 'second' homes. These are used just for part of the year. Many of them are in popular leisure areas, such as near mountains or the coast.

❐ (left) In the wooded lands of Connecticut (USA) small communities can live surrounded by forests. These homes are condominiums, privately owned apartment blocks. You can tell this by the number of parking spaces for each building.

This type of housing is increasingly popular with young professional people. It is less expensive to buy than a single-family home.

By living in the country, and commuting to work in one of the nearby high-tech cities, people can experience many country pursuits like riding, sailing on nearby lakes and walking in the woods.

REVOLUTIONS IN HOUSING

At first they chose to build blocks of apartments that were five stories high. This was the most economical height to build: any higher and the apartment blocks have to be built by different, more costly, methods.

> Social housing was first introduced around the start of the 20th century when governments began to feel that they had a duty to provide housing for the less well off.

But governments soon decided that taller, more massive blocks would be a good way to show everyone the success of the Communist ideas. Giant apartment blocks were built, although the apartments inside were very basic and very small.

Mass production of homes

Europe suffered badly during the long six years of World War II. By 1945 many cities lay in ruins and millions of people were homeless. There had to be a new drive to build new homes quickly. Fortunately, new materials were at hand, and it was discovered that homes, just like machines, could be made up of factory-made concrete parts.

But small, traditional houses could not be made from this material.

❏ (above) The first tower blocks were built in Europe and America in an effort to rehouse those who had lived in old homes. But after they had moved, many people found that they preferred the old houses to the new apartments.

Social housing

Social housing has always been a problem for the governments who subsidise it. Taxpayers want to be sure that their taxes are not being wasted, but despite this social housing is often expensive to maintain, inappropriately designed, and uses the land less efficiently than other forms of housing.

In the 1950s and 60s governments, especially in Europe, felt that tower block living was the way forward for public homes. Nobody ever asked the tenants if they wanted to live in tower blocks, and those who moved in soon discovered that it is not a good place for family living.

Tower blocks are much more expensive to build than houses or low-level apartment blocks. In Europe they were built with huge areas of wasted space between them, and many also suffer from high crime rates.

The situation is very different in East Asia, where tower blocks are still popular. Here the shortage of space forces tower blocks to be built close together. The blocks have not suffered from the problems of crime that have beset those in Europe and North America.

❏ (left) Tower blocks have been more successful in some parts of the world than in others. For example, in East Asia, France, The Netherlands and Switzerland (shown in the picture), they seem to have been well received. In other countries, such as the United States and the United Kingdom, tower blocks have been the least popular type of housing.

❏ (right) Social housing in Chicago (USA). Large areas of the inner city have been cleared away and replaced by these social housing projects. You can just make out some of the older houses in the centre of the picture.

The design and arrangement of the social housing leaves a wasteland of open space. It is very difficult for people to feel part of a community in such housing.

❏ (left) Social housing was built on a grand scale in many Communist countries. In countries like Romania, many well built traditional homes were destroyed in the process.

❏ (above) Many older cities built very large numbers of houses for rent. More recently, some of the oldest apartment blocks have been demolished and the land used once again for smaller, more human housing. Notice how this area in Liverpool (UK) has been redeveloped in a more suburban style, with winding roads and houses with gardens. The old style of rows just shows in the background.

REVOLUTIONS IN HOUSING 45

Architects saw the older houses as belonging to an industrial age of slums and dirt. They wanted to shrug off this old distasteful image for good. In America the skyscraper had captured the imagination, and architects set about rebuilding the homes of their cities in tall concrete apartment blocks.

> Mass production techniques were rushed into action after World War II to replace homes that had been destroyed in Europe and Japan.
>
> Later, the same techniques were applied worldwide. This, more than anything else, has made the world's cities look so similar.

Communist countries across the world were also very enthusiastic about tower blocks of apartments. They had taken on the responsibility of finding homes for all their people. So from Beijing to Moscow, grey uniform slabs of apartment buildings were constructed at such a rate that tens of millions of people each year could be housed.

By the 1970s mass-produced building was becoming important throughout Asia. Japan is 95 per cent mountain, so it makes sense to build in as compact a way as possible. Elsewhere in Asia, governments were faced with huge increases in their populations. In cities where people still have to travel on foot or by bicycle or public transport, cities need to be as compact as possible. Tower blocks provide a way of cramming more people into the centre of a city than by any other means.

The age of concrete tower blocks is not yet over.

Housing the future world

The world's population is already over five and a half billion, by the middle of the next century it might be 10 billion. The only way to try provide homes for this vast number of people is to use mass production techniques.

The pressure on population will be more in some places than others. In Asia it will be severe, and in China (including Hong Kong) and many Southeast Asian countries massive housing plans are already well under way. These changes will make Asia, more than Europe or America, the land of the skyscraper!

❏ (right) These tower blocks in Hong Kong are typical of the style of many prosperous developing cities with high populations.

People here are accustomed to living together and they are not disturbed by high-rise apartment living.

46 REVOLUTIONS IN HOUSING

(left and right) Ideas of what is acceptable for social housing have changed over the decades. Older blocks of apartments are being pulled down and replaced with modern facilities. This is a very expensive process for a government.

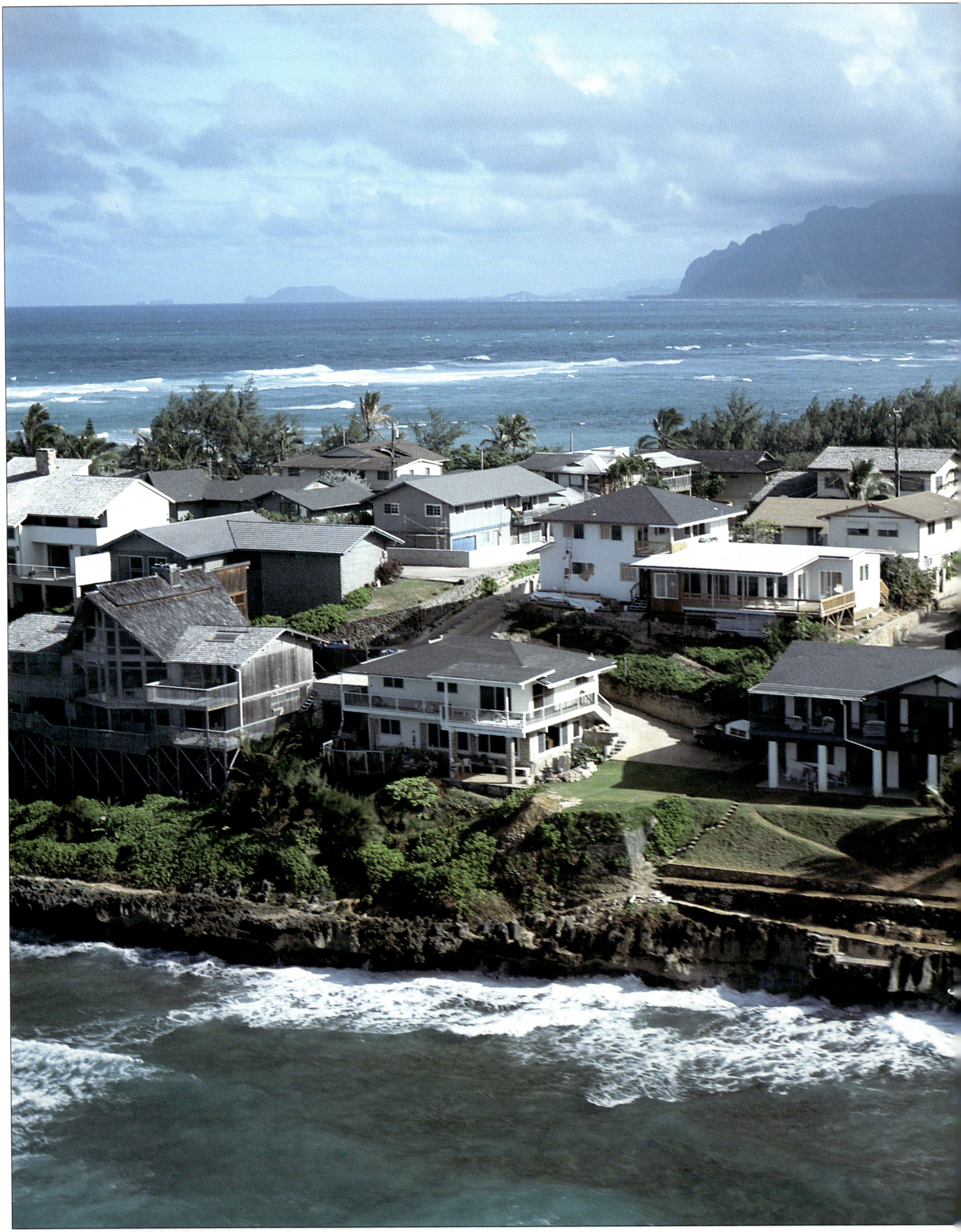

Chapter 4

Homes of the world

Throughout the world homes have to serve the same basic, humble purpose: they must provide shelter for the family. So it may be surprising to find homes of so many different styles in the world.

But differences in climate, traditions and the building materials available have allowed people freedom of design. Today, in an age of concrete, many of the traditional differences are disappearing and the world is in danger of becoming a less interesting place.

The home is not a grand building like a church, a mosque or a temple. Rather it is a modest building in which people live. So while no expense has been spared on the world's grand buildings, homes on the whole have remained simple, their main purpose to create a comfortable and secure place to live.

The home is essentially one or more boxes that are joined together, and little can be done to improve the basic design. This is why people through the ages have concentrated on decorating their homes or furnishing them in special ways, using steep or gently sloping roofs, porches and verandahs, and the many other small things that make a place feel like home.

The variations in homes throughout the world have, in part, been affected by the climate. In a warm wet environment, homes have to keep

❐ (left) These houses by the coast in Hawaii have been built to match the tropical climate. Verandahs, for example, provide shade in the heat of the midday sun and also protect from torrential rainstorms.

HOMES OF THE WORLD 49

people dry; in a hot dry climate houses have to keep people cool; and in a cold place the main purpose of the home is to keep families warm.

Africa and the Middle East

The northern part of Africa has close ties with the Middle East. It is one of the driest places in the world. Summers are ferociously hot and rainfall sparse and unreliable. Trading, rather than farming, has been the mainstay of its people over the centuries. The world's first city was in the Middle East and many desert peoples have traditionally lived in compact villages, towns or cities.

> The housing in Africa, north of the Sahara, developed like that of the Middle East, with closely packed brick homes. South of the Sahara the tradition is for widely spaced huts built using natural materials.

In such places the main building materials are sun-dried mud or adobe. Thick adobe walls are a traditional way of keeping the midday heat from the rooms, and a stone floor is refreshingly cool. In fact, everything about a home is designed to be cool, from the window grills (rather than glass) to the open plan home with its lack of doors.

South of the Sahara two or three months of heavy rainfall are followed by up to five months of drought. To succeed in such places many people have traditionally been pastoralists, looking after herds of animals. They move from one place to another as they seek fresh pastures for their animals. To such people, a complicated home that needs to be protected from attack or vandals has no value, and a number of simple shelters built along the migration route makes far more sense.

But even for those who settle and live in one place there has been no real tradition of town or city living. Cities were introduced by the colonial powers in the 19th century and

Homes in Africa and the Middle East

Africa and the Middle East form the least industrialised part of the world. Here, traditional rural activities that have gone on for centuries can still be found. Only South Africa can be classed as a truly industrial country.

Africa is only now having to come to grips with the pressure on homes that an exploding population brings. The traditional homes are changing, thatched roofs being replaced by tin, mud walls with those of concrete. You see this mostly in the cities, which are made up of small concrete, boxlike homes instead of traditional buildings.

The Middle East is managing to keep many of its fine town and city homes, although modern cities are filled with apartment blocks. In this part of the world where the population is growing fastest of all. The challenge for the future will be to keep the traditional style and still find homes for the millions of people that will soon be starting families of their own.

❐ (above) In Africa, south of the Sahara desert, traditional houses are made in this circular style. The frame is made from woven sticks. The walls are then covered with mud and the roof is thatched. Such homes are quick to build and repair, using local bushes and grasses.

❐ (below) The traditional home has been adapted for modern materials. The thatched roof, for example, has been replaced by longer-lasting corrugated iron.

❐ (right) People who are on the move need only simple shelters. These Maasai homes are used for just a few weeks each year. Afterward the people move on with their animals looking for fresh pastures.

The Maasai build a series of these homes along the route they take each year. They have mud roofs and walls made of sticks. Inside are beds made from wood frames and string. Cooking is done on an open fire.

❐ (below) The Arabs of North Africa and the Middle East developed a traditional style of housing that suited the intense heat of the summer and the need for defence.

The lower part of these houses also served as the town walls. The small windows in the upper, decorated areas help to keep out the heat of the sun. The sunlight is so intense that even small windows will give a well-lit room.

HOMES OF THE WORLD

country people were very reluctant to live in them. Even today, Africa has the smallest proportion of cities to people for any of the populated continents.

Most rural homes are farmhouses. The home serves as a place to sleep overnight and possibly as a place to cook. At all other times people are out in the fields.

Latin America

The colonists who went to Latin America were the Spanish and Portuguese. They had also been influenced in their design by Arab peoples from North Africa, called the Moors.

> When the European colonists arrived in Latin America they had little interest in the long-established local tradition of house building. Instead they brought with them the styles of the Mediterranean. These are still important in Latin American homes today.

The Spanish and Portuguese found a land that already had thousands of years of experience in making permanent homes of stone. Such people as the Mayans who dominated Central America, and the Aztecs and the Incas who lived in the Andes, were highly skilled masons.

But the new colonists were not interested in learning from the native peoples. Traditional home designs were lost and house styles quickly took on patterns of Spain and Portugal.

The New World in Latin America was organised around the city. Homes were built around inside courtyards, in the Roman fashion, with only a small entrance leading from the street. These homes were deigned to be seen from the court, not from the street, and so from the outside they appear plain and uninteresting. Here the main sitting rooms and dining rooms were on the first floor, not at ground level.

Contrasts in Latin America

Latin America shows more contrasts in homes and lifestyles than any other place. While there are millions sheltering in tiny huts called *barrios* on the edges of the great cities, others live in the luxury of grand city houses or in country estates.

Quite separately from the people of the cities are the Indians of the mountains and the rainforests. These people try to live in traditional ways as best they can, but their ways of life and homes are constantly under threat.

❐ (below) The colonial style of many Latin American city dwellings is seen in many streets built in the 19th century. Apartments are above shops. Most are reached through entrances to courtyards.

❐ (left) Many people in Latin America have had to struggle to make their own homes. Many families started out on the city margins and built their houses brick by brick. As money was found, the government made up the roads and brought in electricity. The great variety of home styles that you see in this picture were produced by such gradual improvements.

❐ (right) Latin American families are mainly Roman Catholic and many of the wall decorations have religious themes.
These walls have been reinforced to guard against earthquake damage.

❐ (below) Many settlements high in the Bolivian Andes use stone faced with plaster as their main building material. Here the style is adapted from a traditional Spanish design. Stone is also used for the road surface. Notice that the area seems less wealthy than it might have been in the past. Many of the alterations (such as the bricking up of the window above the door) are far more crude than the original construction.

❐ (above) New developments in Buenos Aires (Argentina) during the 1970s, attempted to bring a new, colourful touch to old cities.

HOMES OF THE WORLD 53

For the most part these colonial styles were too expensive to be copied by the majority of people; they had to look for much simpler styles of home. Their choice was a simple house with a flat roof – the pueblo house – which was originally made from adobe. Although they are now made from concrete or brick, pueblos are still the most common type of home in Latin America.

The United States and Canada

As colonists came from all over Europe to settle in America, they brought their traditional methods of house-building with them. Houses built in the 17th and 18th centuries, from Virginia to New England, from Ontario to Quebec, each reflected the homeland of its makers. People were also keen to keep up with the latest fashions. The Georgian style, for example, soon found its way from Britain to the homes of North America.

> The United States and Canada were home to many Native Americans. But they did not build permanent homes, so when the Europeans arrived there was no native design to copy. Instead, these countries became a melting pot for designs from northern Europe.

But after independence there was a great resistance to styles copied from Britain. Thomas Jefferson (who later became president of the United States), imported the classical styles of the Romans and Greeks by using features such as columns. This style came to be regarded as totally 'American' and was widely used. The best examples of these homes were built on plantations in the south, where cotton and tobacco estate owners were among the richest in the colonies.

As the taste for classic designs faded, new designs, based on the European Gothic period

Varied frame homes in North America

One of the events most important to the making of America occurred in the middle of the 19th century. At this time the American cottage was invented, an idea based on a dream of the rural cottages of New England and the grand houses of the South. It was basically a simple house with easily built wooden frames. Each house was placed centrally in its own plot. This soon became the ideal house of the American middle classes.

The simple frame house was of vital importance in North America because populations were expanding fast and a cheap design that could be constructed with the minimum of skills was badly needed. The American frame house, or cottage, took on many styles, from the two-storey house of the older cities where land was in short supply, to the single-storey bungalow of the countryside where land was cheap and plentiful. Only in the south and west were French and Spanish styles used.

❐ (above) In North America much of the rented housing is provided privately rather than by the government. It still follows the frame house style.

54 HOMES OF THE WORLD

❒ (above) In the north and east the 'colonial' style of housing has been maintained for over 300 years. With so much forest timber available, all houses were made with timber frames and weatherboard exteriors. This house is in Connecticut.

❒ (right) The southern states developed a traditional style that was in part inherited from the French colonial days. The mansion shown here is in Mississippi and it is called an antebellum house. It is typical of the grand houses built during the hey-days of cotton and sugar plantations.

❒ (left) By the time cities began to expand in the west, people began to adopt Spanish designs which were more suited to the warmer climate. This picture is of San Francisco.

❒ (right) The single-family homes built in the south were more influenced by the French style, using shutters and balconies, as in New Orleans (shown here).

HOMES OF THE WORLD   55

of the early middle ages became fashionable. Arched doors and towers were seen on homes of the wealthy. It was a new age that reflected the Industrial Revolution, when ironwork was also in fashion.

But, as in Europe, many cities were faced with the need to build cheaply in small areas. Even the American cottage could not achieve this. As a result American cities, like their European counterparts, saw the invention of the apartment house, with its simple rooms that most people could afford.

Asia

Asia has some of the world's oldest traditions in home design. But although homes were first built where Asia and Europe meet, home design in each continent developed very differently until the age of colonial rule.

Much of Asia is warm and buildings have to protect people from the heat, not the cold.

> The homes of Asia have their own traditions, mainly quite separate from those of Europe. Buildings were designed around the lifestyles and ideas of Buddhism, Hinduism and Islam.

Societies also developed around the village or the trading city, and the effects of the Industrial Revolution largely passed Asia by.

Asia remained a continent of large families, each linked together and living communally. Houses were therefore designed for many families to share, and communal houses are still built this way today.

The Chinese, for example, were very skilled at building and they constructed many fine bridges in stone and one of the world's great wonders – the Great Wall of China – in brick, but buildings, not even temples, were constructed to be long lasting. Most buildings in China were made from wood or bamboo. The home was designed as a frame of wooden

Asia, coping with billions

Asia covers a vast area and is home to more people than anywhere else in the world. Most of the countries still belong to the developing world, yet many have important cultures that date back for thousands of years. So there is a strong sense of tradition in the homes, but the rapidly rising population makes it important to build homes as quickly as possible.

The traditional homes of Asia are still best seen in the countryside, where people largely use natural materials and methods. The need to build quickly has forced city builders to use Western methods, like building tall blocks of apartments. Private transport is not as common as in the West and tower blocks make it possible to house large numbers of people in compact city spaces.

Japan is the most exceptional country in Asia. Its landscape is mountainous so the majority of people are forced to live in crowded cities, and even the wealthy must make do with small apartments.

In contrast, in many Asian cities there are millions of people who can find no home at all, who have to build their own houses. These make the vast shanty towns that are so common today.

❐ (left) Suburban houses in Kyoto, Japan. These single-family homes are the exception rather than the rule in Japan, because land is so scarce. Most people live in apartments.

❐ (below) The Communist government of China has housed hundreds of millions of Chinese. The uniform designs may look uninteresting, but at least everyone has a home.

❐ (left and right) With wages so low and houses in such short supply, hundreds of millions of people are forced to live in self-built shanty homes such as these. The materials are anything that can be found or scavenged including natural materials such as rush and also pieces of plastic sheeting.

❐ (above) Over a billion people in Asia still live in the traditional country way. Traditional houses vary with the needs of the family and the climate.

In China the extended family of grandparents, sons, wives and their children share a large communal courtyard house of stone. These houses have few modern conveniences. In this picture washing is being done in the stream that runs behind the house.

❐ (right) In the tropical forest hills of Thailand, Cambodia and Burma the people make their homes with palm leaf thatch and wood from the local trees. The houses are often on stilts to keep out flooding from the monsoon rains and for overnight shelter of domestic animals such as chickens and pigs.

HOMES OF THE WORLD   57

posts and lintels with bamboo walls in the warm south and adobe walls in the north where winters are cold.

Because tradition was so important, experiment was not encouraged and designs remained the same for centuries.

Japan was, for thousands of years, cut off from the rest of Asia, not just by the China Sea, but also because the Japanese wished to remain apart. Japan has therefore fluctuated from periods when it threw open its doors to the outside world, and absorbed many foreign ideas, and periods when they closed their doors and allowed no external influence. Japanese people became interested in the world being in harmony; they wanted a rustic design but with the dignity of simplicity. This is an important reason why the design of Japanese homes may look plain and uninteresting to Western eyes.

> Australia and New Zealand still have huge expanses of countryside, and the flavour of country living still survives. Their homes are designed to give space and comfort in the long hot summers.

This century Japan has opened itself to the world and taken up a wide variety of Western designs. For example, they have begun to build tower blocks of apartments, a necessary feature since Japan's cities are some of the world's most densely packed.

Australia and New Zealand

Australia has been populated by Aboriginal Australians for about 40,000 years and New Zealand has been peopled by Maoris for about a thousand years. However, these people found little use for permanent housing. The first permanent housing therefore dates from the European colonisation of Australia in 1788 and New Zealand in 1840.

Australian Homes

Unlike cities in many other parts of the world, Australian towns and cities have plenty of room to expand and grow. Therefore, for the past century or so, most Australian homes have been built as separate single-storey homes (bungalows), each surrounded by its own large plot of land. Many Australian homes have wide verandahs to provide shade and circulation of cool air. Few Australians live in apartments (called home units), although the number is growing in inner city areas and near transport routes.

Because Australia is such an enormous country, Australian homes vary from place to place according to the climate. In warm, tropical Queensland, houses are built off the ground so that the air can circulate underneath and cool the home. In southern states where the climate is cooler, most houses are built with brick walls and with tiles or corrugated tin for roofs.

New Australian homes are built with more concern for the energy used in heating and cooling. They make use of features such as solar water heating and are designed without windows on their western sides. Windows here would admit the hot afternoon sunshine through the glass and the rooms would have to use higher levels of air conditioning.

❐ (above) These century-old terraced houses in Geelong, Victoria, show a form of decoration unique to Australia. Notice how each level has a verandah to shade the windows from the direct rays of the sun.

58 HOMES OF THE WORLD

☐ (right) Ground level view of modern suburban housing in Sydney. Notice how the houses have been set in a forest of eucalyptus trees. It was this kind of semi-forested suburban area that was badly affected in the disastrous fires of 1994.

☐ (left) Inner city area in Redfern, Sydney. This consists of terraced houses about a century old.

☐ (above) Family bungalow homes on their garden plots in a suburban area of Bendigo, Victoria.

☐ (below) Family bungalow homes on their garden plots as seen on the ground in Hamilton, Victoria.

HOMES OF THE WORLD 59

The first European settlers in Australia were convicted criminals sent from Britain. Homes for people associated with this early settlement were at first built using local materials such as mud and sticks. But as more people came to settle of their own free will and the wealth of the colony increased, more substantial buildings were constructed using stone and bricks, often modelled on building styles in Britain. In growing cities such as Sydney and Melbourne, terraced housing was built, again modelled on the terraces of British cities.

> Europe is a small, crowded continent, so people need to save space. If they have a large plot they may prefer to have a large garden and a small house.

In New Zealand settlement began with the arrival of British migrants. The cool climate means that homes could be built in British style.

Europe

Europe is a continent of ancient independent countries where there are probably more changes in house style than anywhere else in the world. Partly this is because the climate in the north of the continent is cold and wet, while the south is hot and dry. Snow is common on the main mountain ranges.

❐ (above) A stone-built, single-family home surrounded by a traditional English garden.

European homes: mixing old and new

For many centuries people lived in stone or timber houses in the country. Then the Industrial Revolution came and houses were built in long rows, the countryside disappeared and the country life began to disappear, too.

But people have not given up their love of the country or of the old styles from before the Industrial Revolution. Throughout Europe these old houses give each region its character.

Of course relatively few of these old buildings remain, and most people have to live in modern houses or apartments. But the most popular styles of new home are still those that copy the styles of past, that give a hint of a 'romantic' time, before the Industrial Revolution, that probably exists only in people's imaginations!

❐ (below) The 'half-timbered' frame houses built across England during the 16th and 17th centuries make popular homes, even though the ceilings are low and the rooms small.

❐ (above) The soot-covered homes that were built throughout the Industrial Revolution tell of a time when houses were mass-produced. Few people prefer this style to the rural house.

❐ (left) The characteristic European traditional home is the farmhouse. This German farmhouse was built with space for animals below and people above. Today the barn is used for growing mushrooms.

❐ (right) The weather has played a large part in influencing the style of many European homes. In the Swiss Alps, for example, houses may be cut off from one another by snows. Traditional houses were designed to be self-contained, often having a barn for animals alongside. The sturdy wooden construction was needed to counter fearsome winter blizzards.

❐ (below) Most countries in Europe have had to house many of its people in apartments because there is little room for houses. Houses are far more common in cities of the United Kingdom and southern Europe.

❐ (left) The modern townhouse is built mainly for young professional people. They are built tall so that more homes can be fitted onto the small site. Notice how they have styles which can be compared to the traditional half-timbered home shown on the opposite page.

❐ (below) Many people regard the old houses of the countryside as ideal places to live. In practice they are too small for modern living unless they are greatly adapted.

HOMES OF THE WORLD 61

Despite wars and rebuilding schemes, one of the things that most strikes a visitor from another continent is how old many of the homes seem to be. There is great pride in owning and maintaining a home that might be three, four or even five hundred years old, and many of the villages still have old wooden framed houses in abundance.

Wood was used in forest lands, but stone was used elsewhere, again to give a wide variety of well built homes that have stood the test of time.

Country homes look very different to city homes. The Industrial Revolution brought rows of small, sometimes poorly built, terraced houses that gave European cities a grim feel. There was little love of these small, cramped and insanitary dwellings and many were demolished in the 1960s and 70s. In their place rose great blocks of social housing. But a new feature on the European scene is the modern town house. This, too, is a terraced house, but its outward design is a mixture of styles copied from town houses built before the Industrial Revolution.

Europe is a small, crowded continent, and homes are therefore much smaller and more compact than those in America or Australia. People still have to build up rather than stretch out over valuable land, and Europeans still prefer to have a garden around their house. Flower beds are more common than the wide lawns seen in the United States and Australia.

Homes change from north to south in Europe because southern regions have a warmer climate. Whereas northern homes are designed mainly to keep out the winter cold, southern homes are designed to keep out the heat from the summer sun. The main, and most noticeable, difference in southern Europe is the use of shutters (louvres) on the windows. They allow a breeze to pass through the room, but keep out the worst of the heat and the intense summer sun.

Most of the houses are painted in light colours, to reflect the sun, and are designed around courtyards for privacy. This feature that was taken from Spain and Portugal to Latin America and has influenced the homes there, too.

❑ (right) Southern European city homes have traditionally turned their backs on the hot and dusty streets. Windows have shutters to keep out the heat of the summer sun.

❑ (left) Many homes of southern Europe are painted white to reflect away as much sun as possible.

Glossary

CUL-DE-SAC
The name for a street that is closed at one end. Cul-de-sacs are common in suburban areas because they make for safer and quieter areas for families.

DEVELOPING WORLD
Countries where the majority of people still depend on farming for their living, where wages are poor and there is a lack of advanced technology such as electricity. There are 125 countries classified by the United Nations as coming into this category, including most of those in Asia, Africa and South America.

FLINT
A very hard stone found in the form of nodules and which has traditionally been used to cover the outside of chalk or rubble walls to make them more weatherproof.

RAFTER
The beams in a roof that are used to support the tiles or other roofing materials

RANCH
The name given to a farmhouse particularly in Mexico and the southwestern United States. The name comes from the Spanish word for farmhouse and was introduced into Mexico and then Texas in the 19th century.

SHANTY
The name for an area of poor quality shacks made of flimsy waste materials that has been established illegally by squatters, usually in developing world countries.

SLUM
The name for an area of poor quality houses or apartments that forms part of the inner city, most often in developing world countries.

SPRAWL
The word which is used to describe the spread of houses, roads and other city uses over the countryside. Areas of sprawl appear wasteful to some people because much of the land is garden or other open space.

SOCIAL HOUSING
Housing provided by a public body such as a city council for those people who cannot afford to buy houses or rent homes from private landlords. Social housing has only been provided in this century and because it is very expensive, the amount of social housing is kept as small as possible.

Further reading

This book is one of a series that covers the whole of geography. They may provide you with more information. The series is:

1. **People** of the world, population & migration
2. **Homes** of the world & the way people live
3. The world's **shops** and where they are
4. **Cities** of the world & their future
5. World **transport**, travel & communications
6. **Farms** & the world's food supply
7. World **industry** & making goods
8. The world's **resources** & their exploitation
9. The world's changing **energy** supplies
10. The world's **environment** & conservation
11. World **weather**, climate & climatic change
12. The **Earth** & its changing surface

Index

adobe   12, 17, 21, 50, 54
Africa   50
Age of Discovery   26
air-conditioning   9
Alps   15, 61
America   44, 46, 54
ancient homes   22
Andes   23, 52, 53
antebellum   55
apartment   6, 7, 10, 14, 25, 36, 43, 44, 46, 47, 56, 58, 61
Arab   51, 52
Argentina   53
Asia   30, 44, 46, 56
Australia   10, 30, 31, 58
Aztecs   52

back-to-back homes   32, 34
bamboo   8, 12, 13, 56
brick   8, 16, 18, 60
Britain   54, 60
bungalow   58, 59

Canada   31, 54
caravan   14
castle   24, 25, 26
chalet style   38
China   24, 29, 42, 46, 56
city   7, 22, 32
colonies   28, 54
communal houses   56
Communist   6, 42
commuters   36, 43
concrete   8, 10
condominium   36, 43
cottage   17, 33, 54, 56
countryside   30, 42
courtyard   29, 52
crescent   32
cul-de-sac   38, 63

developing world   12, 18, 63
disaster   11, 14, 18

England   22, 25, 60
environment   14
estate   24, 36, 42, 54

Europe   22, 25, 26, 30, 44, 60, 62
extended family   12

farmhouse   30, 52, 61
flint   16, 63
foundation   8
foyer   30
frame   8, 12, 14, 25, 54, 60
fuel   16

garage   34, 36, 38, 40
garden   29, 35, 36
Gothic   54
Greek   25, 54
gridiron   32

half-timbered   60
hall   30
highway housing   34
historic homes   16, 26, 29
home units   58
homeless   6, 44
Hong Kong   11, 46
hunters and gatherers   23

Incas   52
India   19
industrial city   32
industrial countries   8, 18
Industrial Revolution   32, 56, 60
insulation   16
Iraq   22
Israel   22
Italy   25, 27

Japan   6, 8, 46, 56, 58

keep   24
kitchen   25
Kuwait   8

landlord   6
Latin America   52, 53
leisure   40
limestone   16, 29
lintel   25, 58
Log houses   14
London   5, 28, 30
Los Angeles   5, 34, 36
louvres   62

Maasai   51
Machu Picchu   23
Maoris   58
marina   40
married couples   10

mass-production   46
master builder   28
Mayans   52
medieval system   30
merchants   26
Mesopotamia   21
Mexicans   31
Middle East   8, 24, 50, 51
Mississippi   55
mobile homes   14
monument   22
mortar   17
motor suburb   36
mud-brick   12

Native Americans   23
neighbourhood   8
Netherlands (The)   18
New Brunswick   31
New England   34, 54
New York   30
New Zealand   58
nomad   5
North Africa   51, 52
North America   22, 23, 30, 44, 54
Norway   15

Ontario   54
outer suburbs   38

palace   22
pastoralists   50
Peru   23
pioneers   30
plan   32
plantation   54, 55
poor family   12
Portugal   52, 62
prefabricated   10

quarry   16
Quebec   54
Queensland   58

rafter   8, 63
railway   34
ranch   31, 63
reception room   30
reconstituted stone   16
rectangular house   22
reeds   15
rent   5, 42, 54
ribbon development   34
Roman   25, 54
Romania   45
roof   15, 19
round hut   22

San Francisco   55
sandstone   16
second homes   43
self-build   18
services   9
shanty   18, 63
single-family home   6, 8, 9, 36, 38
single-parent   12
sitting room   30
skyscraper   46
sleeping   8
slum   18, 33, 46, 63
social housing   6, 16, 42, 44, 45, 47, 62, 63
softwood   14
South America   30
Southeast Asia   46
Spain   28, 52, 62
sprawl   36, 63
stone   16, 23, 50, 57, 60
street plan   28
suburb   5, 6, 36, 40
Sumerians   22
Sydney   5, 30, 59, 60

temple   22, 25
tenant   44
terraced house   34, 60
Thailand   57
thatch   15, 50
timber   14, 55
tornado   14
tower block   6, 44, 46, 58
townhouses   7, 16, 61, 62
tropics   12, 14
typhoon   13

United Kingdom   26, 45, 61
United States   14, 30, 54
utility room   36

Venice   27, 29
verandah   9, 13, 49, 58
Victoria   34, 58, 59
villa   25

weatherboard   55
wood   8, 56
wooden house   8, 9, 27, 56, 62
workshop   8
World War II   44

Yurt   5

World Geography **People** of the world, population & migration **Homes** of the world & the way people live The world's **shops** & where they are **Cities** of the world & their future World **transport**, travel & communications **Farms** & the world's food supply World **industry** & making goods The world's **resources** & their exploitation The world's changing **energy** supplies The world's **environment** & conservation World **weather**, climate & climatic change The **Earth** & its changing surface **World Geography** **People** of the world, population & migration **Homes** of the world & the way people live The world's **shops** & where they are **Cities** of the world & their future World **transport**, travel & communications **Farms** & the world's food supply World **industry** & making goods The world's **resources** & their exploitation The world's changing **energy** supplies The world's **environment** & conservation World **weather**, climate & climatic change The **Earth** & its changing surface **World Geography** **People** of the world, population & migration **Homes** of the world & the way people live The world's **shops** & where they are **Cities** of the world & their future World **transport**, travel & communications **Farms** & the world's food supply World **industry** & making goods The world's **resources** & their exploitation The world's changing **energy** supplies The world's **environment** & conservation World **weather**, climate & climatic change The **Earth** & its changing surface **World Geography** **People** of the world, population & migration **Homes** of the world & the way people live The world's **shops** & where they are **Cities** of the world & their future World **transport**, travel & communications **Farms** & the world's food supply World **industry** & making goods The world's **resources** & their exploitation The world's changing **energy** supplies The world's **environment** & conservation World **weather**, climate & climatic change The **Earth** & its changing surface **World Geography** **People** of the world, population & migration **Homes** of the world & the way people live The world's **shops** & where they are **Cities** of the world & their future World **transport**, travel & communications **Farms** & the world's food supply World **industry** & making goods The world's **resources** & their exploitation The world's changing **energy** supplies The world's **environment** & conservation World **weather**, climate & climatic change The **Earth** & its changing surface **World Geography** **People** of the world, population & migration **Homes** of the world & the way people live The world's **shops** & where they are **Cities** of the world & their future World **transport**, travel & communications **Farms** & the world's food supply World **industry** & making goods The world's **resources** & their exploitation The world's changing **energy** supplies The world's **environment** & conservation World **weather**, climate & climatic change The **Earth** & its changing surface **World Geography** **People** of the world, population & migration **Homes** of the world & the way people live The world's **shops** & where they are **Cities** of the world & their future World **transport**, travel & communications **Farms** & the world's food supply World **industry** & making goods The world's **resources** & their exploitation The world's changing **energy** supplies The world's **environment** & conservation World **weather**, climate & climatic change The **Earth** & its changing surface **World Geography** **People** of the world, population & migration **Homes** of the world & the way people live The world's **shops** & where they are **Cities** of the world & their future World **transport**, travel & communications **Farms** & the world's food supply World **industry** & making goods The world's **resources** & their exploitation The world's changing **energy** supplies The world's **environment** & conservation World **weather**, climate & climatic change The **Earth** & its changing surface **World Geography** **People** of the world, population & migration **Homes** of the world & the way people live The world's **shops** & where they are **Cities** of the world & their future World **transport**, travel & communications **Farms** & the world's food supply World **industry** & making goods The world's **resources** & their exploitation The world's changing **energy** supplies The world's **environment** & conservation World **weather**, climate & climatic change The **Earth** & its changing surface **World Geography** **People** of the world, population & migration **Homes** of the world & the way people live The world's **shops** & where they are **Cities** of the world & their future World **transport**, travel & communications **Farms** & the world's food supply World **industry** & making goods The world's **resources** & their exploitation The world's changing **energy** supplies The world's **environment** & conservation World **weather**, climate & climatic change The **Earth** & its changing surface **World Geography** **People** of the world, population & migration **Homes** of the world & the way people live The world's **shops** & where they are **Cities** of the world & their future World **transport**, travel & communications **Farms** & the world's food supply World **industry** & making goods Th